INDONESIA: *Troubled Paradise*

Also by Reba Lewis:

THREE FACES HAS BOMBAY

INDONESIA
Troubled Paradise

REBA LEWIS

ILLUSTRATED AND WITH MAPS

NEW YORK
DAVID McKAY COMPANY, INC.

Library of Congress Catalog Card Number: 62-18710

PRINTED IN GREAT BRITAIN

For
ROGER
with whom I shared
this paradise

Illustrations

facing page

Handsome village women wearing Indonesian national dress on
their way to market in the early morning 64

A typical Javanese bullock cart 65

Child working in the rice fields 65

A porter takes his vegetables to market, carrying them on a
shoulder pole which was introduced to Indonesia by the
Chinese hundreds of years ago 80

A farmer ploughing his rice fields with bullocks 80

Sumiyati finishing a new *batik* 81

At the stamp bazaar 81

Administration building of Airlangga University 112

Girl students parading during the West Irian crisis 112

The Hindu Museum in the village of Trawulen. The museum
is an exact reproduction of a fourteenth-century building 113

Tenggerese at the Kasada ceremony with offerings for the
Hindu gods of Mount Bromo 113

The sinuous, winding rice terraces of Bali 128

Sculptured head of a girl in the Hindu Museum, Trawulen 129

Elaborate inscription on the head stone of the grave of Ibrahim
Malik, one of the first holy men to expound the doctrine of
Islam in Indonesia 129

Part of a Buddhist bas-relief at Borobudur depicting musicians
and dancing girls 129

Balinese cremation ceremony. Women carrying bones to be
blessed by the Brahman priest 160

The wooden cows inside which the bones have been placed
burning at the auspicious hour 160

The Barong discussing some of his problems with the monkey 161

Two Balinese children who take the main dancing rôles in the
Barong drama 176

Performance of the famous Ketjak dance of Bali 176

President Sukarno relaxing with friends 177

Dr. Soendoro nails his name to the mace of the University after
being promoted 177

MAPS

The Indonesian Archipelago *page* 8

Java: The main cities, towns and roads 23

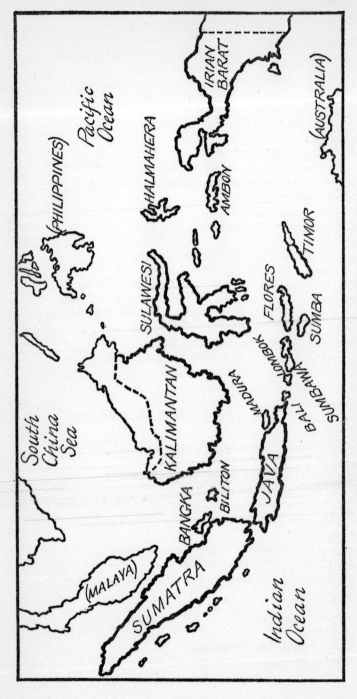

The Indonesian Archipelago and neighbouring countries

Chapter One

WE WERE LIVING in Lucknow, a romantic city in northern India, which had long been a centre of Muslim culture. It was the month of June, 1957, and the heat, like a thick woollen blanket, had wrapped the city in its embrace. Throughout the day the sun shone, its merciless rays withering all living things. And when night came there was no respite. The hours dragged by wearily as though time itself had become exhausted.

My husband had been assigned to Lucknow by the World Health Organization to act as a consultant for the Central Drug Research Institute. The Institute was housed in the Chatter Manzil Palace, a lovely retreat built by the famous Nawab Ghaziuddin Haider on the bank of the sweet-flowing Gomati River. An English visitor, in the 1850s, was so struck by its charm that she wrote to a friend: "Such a palace—the only residence I have coveted in India: Don't you remember reading in the Arabian Nights, Zobeide bets her Garden of Delight against the Caliph's Palace of Pictures? I am sure this was the Garden of Delight."

Compared to any place else the palace was deliciously cool because of its thick walls and deep underground cellars. My husband looked forward to spending his mornings there, where he and his fellow scientists were surrounded by the echoes of those days when the Chatter Manzil was used only for pleasure and not for work, and the great halls resounded to the bells of the kathak dancers.

The monotony of the Lucknow summer was suddenly broken when my husband said: "I have been given a new assignment. We are going to Surabaja."

I tried to look knowledgeable, but perhaps because of the intense heat, I did not succeed. All my mind conjured up about Surabaja was a haunting lyric, sung by Lotte Lenya, called "Surabaja Johnny"; a sad story of a handsome sailor from Surabaja, who had sailed to Rangoon where he had broken the heart of a beautiful Burmese girl. Having lived in Rangoon for one adventurous year, that part of the song was quite clear to me—but Surabaja remained a mystery. Finally, I asked my husband: "Where is Surabaja?"

Instead of answering, he replied: "If you know the location of Indonesia, I can tell you."

Then and there I decided not to pursue the geographic aspect of the problem; instead I inquired: "And what will you do in Surabaja?"

"I will be the visiting Professor of Pharmacology at the Fakultas Kedokteran, which is affiliated with Airlangga University. From what I have learned, the Indonesians are very anxious to get professors from the W.H.O., as they urgently need more physicians. At present they have only one doctor for every sixty thousand persons."

"That figure sounds impossible," I protested. "Even India has one doctor for six thousand people . . ."

"Perhaps I am wrong, but we will learn more when we get there."

The next morning I went to the library at the University of Lucknow and then to all the bookshops in the city hunting for information. There was not a single book about Indonesia, so I was reduced to reading the dry-as-dust account of the country in the encyclopaedia. I found that Surabaja is a seaport and an industrial city, located in East Java, with a population of a million and a half; and that Java is the most important and most densely populated of the 3,000 islands comprising the Indonesian Archipelago. Close to sixty million people, out of a total population of nearly ninety millions, live on that one island.

Indonesia has a land area about twice as large as that of Texas or six times that of Great Britain. If Indonesia were superimposed on a map of the Atlantic Ocean, with its westernmost island on the site of New York, its eastern extremity would reach as far as French West Africa. The main islands are Sumatra, Borneo, Java, Celebes, Bali, Flores and Timor—but after Indonesian independence, the name of Borneo was changed to Kalimantan and the Celebes became Sulawesi.

Located on both sides of the Equator, Indonesia has a tropical but fairly equable climate. Like India, the state of the weather is determined by the monsoon. South of the Equator, on the islands of Java and Bali, the East monsoon generally lasts from April until November, and the West monsoon, which is accompanied by rains, from December until March.

Of course, I had heard about a few of the main islands. But, like everyone else, my fragments of knowledge were spun from the odds and ends I had read in various novels: the fine coffee of Java; the pungent cloves of Ambon; the bare-breasted women of Bali and the headhunters of Borneo. But I knew nothing about Indonesia as a whole, even though it is the sixth most populous country in the world, and in South-East Asia second only to India in size and population.

My lack of knowledge was understandable, for until 1945 when Indonesia achieved independence, the average person thought of the East Indies as a group of unrelated islands that had been brought under the tender and protective wing of the Dutch. Even the name Indonesia was not used, except by a few learned historians and members of the Indonesian nationalist movement. Officially, the islands were called *Netherlands Indies*.

I felt slightly compensated for my own ignorance when just before leaving Lucknow my husband received a letter from a friend in the United States who wrote: "I was surprised to hear that you are going to Indonesia. I thought your destination was Java."

When I read that most Indonesians are Muslims, I immediately visualized Surabaja as being like Lucknow. Part of the vision was a pleasant one for Lucknow is an interesting city with its historic palaces and impressive mosques. But its beauty is marred by the poverty of the people, the majority of whom live in hovels and dress in rags. And its charm is spoiled because many women are still forced to wear a "burqa"; an ugly black cloak which covers them from head to foot and is symbolic of their subjugation.

The information which I acquired about Indonesia could be compared to an X-ray rather than to a portrait; the bones were there but the features, the personality and the beauty were missing. In actuality, Surabaja was to prove entirely different from Lucknow.

It was the beginning of August when we landed at Djakarta, the capital of the nation and the largest city in the Archipelago. Due to some misunderstanding, no one met us at the airport. Fortunately, the hostess of our KLM plane, a Dutch girl who spoke perfect English, noticed our plight and suggested that we go to the Transaera Hotel where, if we were lucky, we might be accommodated. But how to get there? We did not see a single taxicab.

"You must go by betjak," the hostess explained. "There are more than 40,000 betjaks in Djakarta, so it is never difficult to get one. You will need two, one for yourselves and one for all your luggage."

She signalled two betjaks, which were very much like the pedi-cabs of Lucknow, but more gaily decorated with pictures of ships and buffaloes painted on the sides. The betjak consists of a double seat, mounted on a pair of cycle wheels placed in front of the rear half of a bicycle on which a man sits and pedals. The passengers are in the most vulnerable position should an accident occur, and possibly because the driver realizes this, he throws all caution to the winds.

Every betjak has a name and the two that stopped for us were *Krisna* and *Ardjuna*. Though the spellings were unfamiliar, the names of Krishna and Arjuna were well known to us. After four years in India, Krishna, the God of Love, and Arjuna, the hero of the *Mahabharata*, seemed like old friends. I had become enough of a Hindu to consider this an auspicious beginning.

The betjak drivers pedalled quickly, weaving in and out of the heavy traffic with considerable skill, while the two rubber bands, stretched under the seat near the ground, began vibrating, so that we could listen to their pleasant hum as we rode through the city streets.

So this was Djakarta, an historic sea-port whose harbour princes, as early as the fifteenth century, were trading with other countries. These princes, who controlled the port, lived in different sections of the city with their own artisans, workers, poets, dancers and officials. It was to them that the Dutch paid homage when they came, bribing them to grant concessions and gradually taking over control of the main avenues of trade.

As the power of the Dutch became more entrenched, they tried to change the character of the city by digging canals and building small houses with red roofs and tiny, narrow windows, which are still standing today, incongruous structures in a climate where the temperature rarely dips below ninety degrees.

Over the years, the Dutch officials found that it was unhealthy to stay in Djakarta, so they moved to the outskirts where they built Javanese-type houses; low-lying villas with broad expanses of court-yard, which proved not only more beautiful but more sensible. In the meantime, the poor people crowded into the interior of the city, each nationality—Javanese, Chinese and Arab—having its own quarters and following its own customs.

After Indonesia achieved independence and the new headquarters of the Republican Government were moved from Jogjakarta to Djakarta, in 1950, thousands of workers, job-seekers, hangers-on, demobilized army youths and civilians flocked into the city, filling every nook and cranny. The price of real estate soared. Djakarta became a boom town.

As we whirled through the city, I was immediately struck by the women. Not one wore a burqa. Not one had her face covered.

Gaily dressed, some in western frocks and others in Indonesian national dress, they seemed full of vigour, life and happiness. The men were not as clearly etched in that first impression, but seeing the women I knew that I would like Indonesia, and that I would not suffer the sense of depression I had in Lucknow whenever a shrouded figure passed, announcing by her black costume the sorrows of her existence.

If the women were lovely to see, the city was not. We were dismayed by its unkempt appearance. One felt it to be in a state of decay, and this impression was heightened by the smell emanating from the main canal that runs through the middle of the city like a muddy ribbon. In this canal the poor people were bathing, washing their clothes and obtaining drinking water. They were also using it for other essential bodily functions, so that from the aesthetic point of view it was not pleasant and from the health point of view, dangerous.

Arriving at the Transaera Hotel we were delighted to find it so clean and brightly lit. The manager agreed to let us stay and our luggage was taken into one of the small pavilions. The hotel was built in the shape of an L, and each room was a self-contained unit, with a large terrace in front and a bedroom and bath in the back. The terrace was furnished as though it were the living-room, and all would have been perfect except it was not screened, so during the day we were plagued with flies and at night by mosquitoes.

After having washed we decided to take dinner. The dining-room in the main building was very crowded. We could not find a table for two, so we asked permission to share one with a Dutchman, tall and blond with blue eyes, typical of his countrymen. He asked us if this were our first visit to Djakarta and when we said yes, he replied with the nostalgic remark that is so often heard from Europeans living in Asia today. He said: "You should have seen Djakarta before the war. It was a wonderful city."

He reminded us of the Englishman who remarked, "Oh, if you could only have seen Rangoon before," and the Frenchman who sighed, "C'est dommage. You should have been in Saigon before."

"Yes, Djakarta must have been quite different," my husband said, "but what surprises me is the number of Dutch people we see here now. I thought that after the revolution the Dutch had gone home."

"Some of us stayed," he answered. "You see, we were only toppled politically. Economically, we still have great influence, and unless

13

you Americans elbow us out, we will continue to play an important role in the development of the country. We are needed here. After all, we did a damn good job for three hundred years and they would be lost without our help."

Just as he had said, we found there were a great many Dutch companies and banks in Djakarta. The Dutch language was spoken everywhere, not only by the Dutch people but by most of the Indonesians we met. Many of the newspapers were published in Dutch. There were a number of Dutch schools and at the University there were several Dutch professors. But the main strength of the Dutch in Indonesia remained in the field of transport, for the Royal Dutch Packet Shipping Lines still ruled the waves between the islands as it had done for almost seventy years, and the air routes between Indonesia and other countries were monopolized by the KLM.

Later when we were talking about this with an Indonesian government official, he was quite bitter.

"We are still not free," he declared. "Political independence is not enough if you are chained to another country economically. And at the present time we are bound to Holland just as we have been for three hundred years. The Dutch," he continued, "first came to Indonesia in 1596, and they were amazed to find a land that was so prosperous and where such a high degree of civilization had been attained. We knew how to cultivate rice on irrigated fields and how to mill sugar. And even then we were engaged in trade with India, China, Japan, Turkey and Persia.

"Realizing the tremendous possibilities of the islands various Dutch, trading companies amalgamated to form the Dutch East India Company. Backed by the approval of the Dutch Government, the Company began its penetration of Indonesia. And do you know what the Company did first?"

"No," I said, noticing how tense he had become, as though the events he was relating happened only yesterday.

"The Company decided to build a fort on Java. The Javanese rulers resisted with all their might, knowing full well what this would mean. The powerful ruler of Banten wanted to know what the Dutch intended to do, 'with all these castles in the Indies,' declaring that 'it was odious to the Javanese to have castles in their land'.

"But the ruler of Djakarta, or Djayakerta, as it was known then, was a weak man and allowed the Dutch to build a fortified town. For having done this he was cursed by the other Javanese sultans, who declared that he was 'a heathen', and, 'a man who did not put his trust in Mohammed.'

"The Dutch called their walled city Batavia, after an ancient German tribe from whom they claim to be descended. It was from Batavia that they sent their expeditionary forces to conquer the outer islands. Gradually, the Dutch armies subdued one island after another; the Moluccas; Sulawesi; Kalimantan; Sumatra; Bali; Lombok; Flores and even Timor, where Captain Bligh ended his historic four-thousand-mile voyage after the mutiny on the *Bounty*.

"Once these islands were in their control, they kept a never-ending stream of natural resources flowing from our land to theirs. While one out of every six Hollanders depended upon the Indies for a live-lihood and fabulous fortunes were made, we who lived here and worked to supply this wealth were, in the words of your President Roosevelt, 'ill-housed, ill-clothed and ill-fed.'

"And so," he said, shaking his head ruefully, "our Javanese legend with all its portent of sorrow and evil came to pass. For among us there had been a prediction that, 'A strange nation shall come from far away; white in colour; wholly clothed, yea even the hands and feet; having cat's-eyes and large noses; eating pork; which shall possess these lands and destroy the Mohammedan faith'."

"But this period has passed," I said, feeling deeply the impact of his remarks.

"Not entirely, because we are still tied to the Dutch," he replied. "I always feel that Djakarta, even though its traditional name has been restored, is haunted by the ghosts of yesterday, who wander about weeping over the cruel fate they suffered, so for this reason, I agree with those members of Parliament who think that we should move the capital to another location."

When we wandered about Djakarta, we never met any of our friend's weeping ghosts, but there was an atmosphere of sadness, per-haps because the city is so old, or perhaps because I was influenced by the diary of Captain Cook, who having landed in Batavia in 1770, declared that "in this country, to delay is death".

The only new section of the city is Kabajoran, where foreigners and government officials live. It has been built for the exigencies of the present and there is no sign of city planning. Each house reflects the taste and wealth of the owner. Far away from Kabajoran is the Chinese part of the city, Glodok. The Chinese of Djakarta live in a world of their own. Their houses, some of which were built in the seventeenth century, are pressed together like tiny tea sandwiches. Cheek by jowl are furniture makers; leather workers; goldsmiths; jewellers; tailors; dentists; and doctors.

Not far from Glodok, in the harbour area, known as Tandjung Priok, are the Arab quarters, ancient abodes facing the sea. The shutters of these houses are often intricately carved, but never representative of any living thing, for the Arabs are strict Muslims, following the Koranic prohibition that life may not be reproduced in art. Slender and sharp-nosed with magnificent eyes, the Arabs have a reckless air. Their women are also handsome, and although they may be restricted to a special area within the house, once they emerge they are free. If an Arab woman were to be seen anywhere in Indonesia covered by a burqa, she would be subject to so much ridicule that she would return home at once.

But what we found most astounding about Djakarta were the kampungs. According to the Indonesian dictionary, a kampung may be "a district, a town quarter or a slum"; while a perkampungan is "a complex of dwellings of the lower classes of the population". All of these definitions may be correct but none of them emphasize the character of the kampung, which is really a village within a city.

Over a period of many years, country people have been moving to the towns. This movement from the rural areas to the cities is as marked in Indonesia as in all other countries of the world. Finding it impossible to obtain decent housing the newcomers have either rented or squatted on any parcel of land that was available. As soon as they could, they built their dwellings. Some were well constructed, but the majority were thrown together from a collection of straw, bamboo and scrap iron without any adequate sanitary arrangements.

But these kampungs differ from city slums for they are neat and clean and manage to avoid the sordid look that characterizes the poor sections of other cities. The inhabitants take pride in keeping the lanes swept and many of them plant flowers around their dwellings. There is hardly a house that does not have a bird. These birds are kept in cages and the cages are hoisted upon poles that are often fifteen or twenty feet high so the birds, at least, have the illusion of freedom. Other dwellers allow their birds to fly away for they are trained to return at the sound of a certain hand-clap, and in the evening, as the sun is going down, one can hear the sound of soft clapping in the kampungs.

The reason the people in the kampungs lead a better life than the poor of towns in other Asian countries, is because the country people do not give up the co-operative system which is a part of the way of life when they live in the villages. This means that in each kampung there is a governing council, and it takes care of those who are ill or are in financial difficulties. The inhabitants appear to be independent and happy. The women dress in colourful sarongs and many wear flowers in their hair, and their laughter sounds like the sweet chimes of a clock. Angry voices are rarely heard in the kampung, not only because the Indonesians are slow to anger but because their way of life is not so individualistic that each must fight for himself and in doing so hurt someone else.

In contrast to the harmony and orderliness that seems to be characteristic of the kampungs, the main part of Djakarta is in complete disorder. The streets are narrow, and at the rush hour, when people are going to work or returning home, it is almost impossible to drive a car. The road is obstructed by people walking, betjaks, bicycles, pony carts or beef cattle being marched through the centre of the town to the slaughter houses. Adding to the congestion are the numerous grade crossings where trains often block the traffic for more than an hour. But the people do not seem to mind and it is only the foreigners who become impatient.

In most capital cities of the world there is usually one building of historic importance or of great beauty. Thus, in Washington D.C., there is the Lincoln Memorial; in Paris, the Eiffel Tower; in Moscow, the Kremlin; in New Delhi, the Red Fort and in Rangoon, the Shwedagon Pagoda. But in Djakarta the public buildings are only reminders of the Dutch. As yet the Indonesians have been hesitant to erect new buildings for they are not sure whether Djakarta will remain the capital of the nation.

But if there is not a single imposing edifice in the city, there is a man who dominates its life. That man is President Sukarno, whose picture can be seen prominently displayed in every public place. The President and Djakarta are inseparably linked. It is his city and his capital. He is both the architect and the guardian of Indonesian freedom. Unlike Jawaharlal Nehru, who must acknowledge his great debt to the founder of Indian independence, Mahatma Gandhi, or U Nu, who is overshadowed by the great Burmese patriot, Aung San, Sukarno stands alone.

Sukarno, whose father was Javanese and whose mother was Balinese, has no first name. There is a story, probably apocryphal, that when he

17   B

was a small boy he was called Krishna. But as he grew up, his father thought this was not proper. Sukarno's mother agreed to change his name but said that she must be allowed to choose the new one. And so she called him Sukarno, which has a Sanskrit origin and means, "the doer of good deeds."

Born in Surabaja, in 1901, Sukarno attended the Hogere Burger School. In the early 1920s he became immersed in politics and joined the Young Java Movement. He contributed articles to a national journal, the *Utusan Hindia*, taking as a pen name, that of Bima, second of the five Pandava brothers in the *Mahabharata*, famed for his strength and honesty. After leaving Surabaja, Sukarno entered the Bandung Technical School where he became an engineer. But his main interest was in the nationalist movement and while a student he organized, in 1926, the Bandung Study Club and edited a newspaper dedicated to the ideals of Young Indonesia.

In 1927, as an outgrowth of the Bandung Study Club, he organized the Partai Nasional Indonesia (the Indonesian Nationalist Party). Because of his outspoken demands for Indonesian independence he was arrested in 1928 and sentenced to four years' imprisonment. He conducted his own defence and this was later published as a pamphlet entitled, *Indonesia Accuses*, written in the tradition of Emile Zola.

While in prison his sentence was reduced and he was released in 1930. But as he resumed his political activities he was re-arrested in the same year and exiled to Flores, one of the Lesser Sunda Islands. From that time on, until 1942, with the exception of two years, he was continuously incarcerated by the Dutch. He was freed by the Japanese when they conquered Indonesia. And after their capitulation to the Allies, it was Sukarno who delivered the proclamation of Indonesian independence on August 17th, 1945.

The day before we left Djakarta we heard the President speak. It was August 17th, 1957, the twelfth anniversary of Indonesian independence. He was standing at the top of the steps of Merdeka Palace, "merdeka" being an Indonesian word of great significance as it means freedom. The President looked very handsome in his powder-blue uniform and his black velvet "pitji" which is a pointed cap, made of silk in Sumatra and of velvet in Java, and is worn only by Muslim men.

The morning was brilliant and the crowds that had gathered to hear Sukarno were in a holiday mood. Speaking forcefully and effectively —we had already been told that he had the reputation of being the nation's finest orator—the President immediately captured the attention of his audience. From the English text which had been given to us we were able to follow his speech, and it soon became evident that the theme he was developing would have great bearing on the political future of the country.

His thesis was that western parliamentary democracy had failed in Indonesia. It had not only failed but it had boiled over "into anarchy". Bitterly castigating what he called, "free-fight liberalism democracy," Sukarno declared that he was no longer prepared to accept this type of democracy "without guidance and without discipline" which was "not in keeping with the identity of the Indonesian people and the mental outlook of the Indonesian nation".

Democracy without discipline had, in Sukarno's words, "turned into a chatter-box democracy," incapable of any effective action. Furthermore, it had enabled a few people to exploit the many. Nor did the President feel that western democracy could any longer be depended upon to offer new or constructive ideas for the building of a happier or more prosperous Indonesia.

Then Sukarno asked the members of his spellbound audience if they were in favour of clinging to this "free-fight liberalism", which had not only caused, "sixteen cabinet crises in the short course of twelve years", an average of one crisis every eight months, but had brought the nation to the brink of financial bankruptcy. In addition it had fostered corruption, poisoning the Armed Forces. "At present," Sukarno declared, "we are still dazed by the crisis in the Army."

Nor had western democracy been a force in improving the cultural development of the country. On the contrary, it had fostered the growth of third-rate films, rotten comic books and the "madness of rock-and-roll". Over the years, the President declared, there had been a decline in national consciousness and in the national spirit, especially among the youth who were influenced by the West and who had become "crazy about the mambo and the rock-and-roll".

"We have not," Sukarno said, "been witnesses to the melodiousness of pure Indonesian music, but to the din of swing and jazz and mambo-rock. We have not been witnesses to the creative power of excellent Indonesian literature but to a flood of comics."

To achieve stability the political system had to be revised and another substituted which would be in keeping with the identity of the nation and which would have one aim, "A society based on social justice." To bolster his point of view, the President quoted from French, Dutch, Latin and English sources, speaking each language fluently. His audience listened quietly and intently. When he was finished there was a round of polite applause.

For a newcomer it was not possible to evaluate the speech nor to comprehend the basic philosophy motivating the President's thinking. That he felt western democracy had failed was obvious, but whether the solution he proposed of "guided democracy" would relieve Indonesia of the political and economic instability which had afflicted the nation since independence, remained to be seen.

In the meantime, I, like everyone else, felt the magnetism and strength of the President's personality. And my last lingering impression was that of Sukarno, clearly outlined in the sunlight, impeccably groomed, appealing to a large group of gaily dressed people who stood in front of his Merdeka Palace.

Chapter Two

THE FOLLOWING DAY we left the capital and started on our way to Bandung where we were going to halt for the night. We were driving our new green and white Metropolitan which we had ordered in Singapore and which was delivered to us in Djakarta at the office of the United Nations the morning that we planned to start on our journey.

The drive was lovely and it did not take long for us to cover the first fifty kilometres. Entering Bogor, we saw a beautiful estate. On the well-kept lawn deer were grazing, and in the background we could see an enormous country home. This was built more than two hundred years ago by the aristocratic Dutch Governor-General, Baron Willem van Imhoff, who called it Buitenzorg, which like "sans souci" means "without care".

The name was a suitable one for during the reign of the Dutch Governor-Generals, Buitenzorg was the scene of many glamorous parties. The wealthy burghers from Batavia journeyed to Bogor for riding, hunting and dancing. They brought with them friends, mistresses or wives, and sometimes all three. According to one highly placed English observer, who had attended one of the functions at Buitenzorg, the Dutch women were no beauties. Looking down his long English nose he commented, "The elder Dutch ladies were in a class not yet described in Europe. The principal mark to know them by is their immense size. The whole colonial sex runs naturally to fat, partly from over-feeding, partly from want of exercise."

But during the eighteenth and nineteenth centuries few Dutch women had come to the Indies. The Dutch men mingled with the women of Java, and because of this, the period came to be known as Indische, neither pure Dutch nor pure Indonesian. This Indische society was rich and indolent. The men were heavy drinkers, enjoying the delicious indigenous brew called Tuak, and smoking good Havana cigars which could be purchased for ten dollars a thousand. Their Javanese women, richly dressed and surrounded by servants, were addicted to chewing betel. "Even when they went to church they were accompanied by slave girls who carried the prayer book, the betel

21

box and the spittoon. The last equipment was often made of gold or silver but it remained a spittoon."

The Indische society was shaped like a pyramid. At the bottom were the slaves, some of whom were sailors who had been captured at sea; some were Javanese taken in predatory raids; but most of them were imported from the outer islands. According to Captain Cook, the slaves were beaten—with a ghastly weapon; a thick piece of bamboo split down many times, called a rattan. It was almost a handful of knives and fetched blood at every stroke.

Then came the free Indonesians who were not much better off, for the criminal code which the Dutch invoked against them was as severe as for the slaves. They were branded, and broken at the wheel and even impaled alive without mercy.

Far above them were the Dutch clerks, craftsmen and soldiers, who had come to the Indies seeking their fortune. They too were roughly handled. The shoemakers for the East India Company were forced to finish one pair of shoes a day under penalty of being jailed. Clerks who did not do their job well were beaten with a thick stick. Theirs was no easy life and many died of malaria, of dysentery and of homesickness.

At the top of the pyramid were the officers; members of the governing hierarchy; and the merchants, who went to Buitenzorg for weekends when invited by the Governor. They were the pampered élite.

Today, the palace of Buitenzorg belongs to President Sukarno, and is still the scene of gala parties. But because the President does not approve of western dancing, guests must learn the Indonesian dance, Sarampang Duabelas, which is difficult for anyone who is a bit stiff or old, a category to which Sukarno does not belong.

As the palace was closed we went instead to the Bogor Botanical Garden, which is one of the most famous in the world, both for its beauty and its scientific importance, as almost every species of tropical vegetation is represented.

Afterwards we visited the Veterinary Institute and its Pharmacology Laboratory, which interested my husband, because the pharmacologists there were testing the purity of the Rauwolfia plant which grows in Indonesia as well as India. *Rauwolfia serpentina*, with a history more romantic than that of a film star, was first used in ancient India for mental illness. In our time it was discovered to be of value in the treatment of high blood pressure and then later found to be effective in the therapy of insanity. So after a thousand years, the circle was completed.

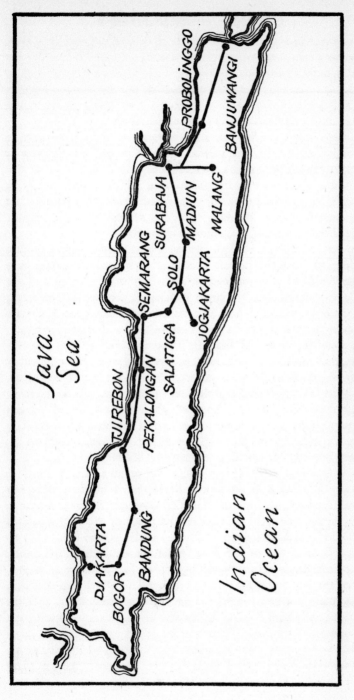

Java: The main cities, towns and roads

The Veterinary Institute was excellently maintained and there were a number of women working there, wearing pristine white frocks but with flowers in their hair. As we were leaving the Institute I noticed on the wall an old, faded photograph of the American naturalist, Dr. Thomas Horsfield, who had worked in Java during the nineteenth century, studying the flora and fauna of the island.

Leaving Bogor, the drive became spectacularly beautiful as we were winding our way through paddy fields, tea gardens, and forests of cinchona, the tree whose bark is used for the production of quinine. We were driving towards the mountain area, which at the summit or "puntjak", is over four thousand eight hundred feet high. From there we planned to go to Bandung, which is situated on a plateau surrounded by a series of high, volcanic mountains.

Bandung is a large, modern city with broad avenues, trams, office buildings and many factories. The hotel where we stayed was built in the American style—a mass of steel, glass and chrome—and exceedingly comfortable. The night we arrived a gala affair was being held in the ballroom. A new film, called *Tiga Dara*, concerned with the antics of three sisters, had just been released and some clever publicity man had invited all the girls living in Bandung who had two sisters, thus forming a triumvirate, to come and participate in a contest where the prettiest and most talented three sisters would be chosen. The ballroom was crowded with sisters, none of whom seemed to be shy, as they walked out into the spotlight without hesitation. There, they stood together and sang one or two of the hit songs from *Tiga Dara*. At midnight, the lucky three still had not been chosen, so we went to bed without knowing which group had won.

Early the next morning we visited the quinine factory which is probably the largest in the world. More than a hundred years ago several Dutch experts from the Botanical Garden in Bogor had gone to South America in order to discover the secret of growing cinchona trees. The botanists returned with some seedlings, and from then on quinine became one of the most important products of the Indies. From the beginning of the twentieth century, Java had a virtual monopoly on the growing of the cinchona trees and the Dutch, together with the Germans, formed a cartel for the sale of quinine which kept the price artificially high. During the Second World War, the Japanese cut off the supply of quinine. Because allied armies had to fight much of the war in malarious areas, it became necessary to find a substitute for this important drug. Several synthetics were produced, many of them

24

better than quinine in curing malaria, and when the war was over, quinine no longer had to be used. So now, the problem faced by the factory at Bandung is to find other uses for quinine and its by-products.

Leaving the factory we wandered around the city. Everywhere we saw luxurious homes and fine swimming pools. Because of its relatively mild climate, the Dutch had built their finest homes in Bandung, and for generations lived there in opulence and security, unmindful of the danger that was threatening their seemingly firm position. And it was precisely in Bandung that they faced their greatest humiliation, for there in March of 1942, the Dutch Commander-in-Chief of the Allied Forces on Java, Lieut.-General Ter Poorten, surrendered to the Japanese.

With the Dutch surrender, the people of Indonesia felt themselves abandoned. Before this it had been believed that the Dutch were going to make a deal with the Japanese, whereby they would continue to control the Indies, with the Japanese only as nominal victors. This had been the pattern in Indo-China, where the French had made such an agreement with the Japanese. In Indonesia, however, it soon became obvious that this was not the case, but the suspicion remained that rather than give arms to the people, the Dutch preferred a Japanese victory.

Describing the suffering which took place during the Japanese occupation, Soetan Sjahrir, the first Prime Minister of Indonesia, wrote in his *Political Manifesto*:

"When the Netherlands Indies Government surrendered to the Japanese, our unarmed population fell prey to the harshness and cruelty of Japanese militarism. For three and a half years our people were bent under a cruelty which they had never before experienced. Our people were treated as worthless material to be wasted in the process of war. From the lowly stations of those who were forced to accept compulsory labour and slavery and those whose crops were stolen, to the intellectuals who were forced to propagate lies, the grip of Japanese militarism was universally felt."

For this Sjahrir declared, "Dutch colonialism is responsible in that it left our seventy million people at the mercy of Japanese militarism without any means of protecting themselves since they had never been entrusted with fire-arms or with the education necessary to use them."

After independence, it was in Bandung that resurgent Asian and African nationalism made its imprint on the world. The building in which this meeting was held in April of 1955, is a spectacular white colonnaded structure. Eminent statesmen of twenty-nine countries met there to consider the manifold problems facing the Asian and African nations. Among the most prominent were Nehru and Chou En-lai.

Nehru was extremely popular because during 1949 when the Dutch attempted an all-out military conquest of Indonesia he called a conference in New Delhi whose members—Afghanistan, Australia, Burma, Ceylon, Egypt, Ethiopia, India, Iran, Iraq, Lebanon, Pakistan, Philippines, Saudi Arabia, Syria and Yemen—presented a strongly worded resolution to the Security Council that the Dutch action constituted a threat to world peace and therefore the Government of the Netherlands should be forced to recall its troops. "The Dutch action in Indonesia," Nehru exclaimed at the time, "is an astounding thing which the new spirit of Asia will not tolerate."

The Bandung Congress was not the first attended by Asian delegates for as early as 1926 Asian opinion was voiced at the non-official International Conference for Peace, but it was the voice of a supplicant not of an equal. The humble memorandum presented there, protested:

"In the imagination of European thinkers, the world seems to be confined to the areas inhabited by European races. The vast Continent of Asia, containing as it does, some of the most ancient civilizations, and Africa, with its particular problems, do not come into the picture at all. This, we submit with all humility, is a wrong point of view."

But if Bandung were not the first conference attended by Asians, it was the first where both African and Asian delegates were present and western powers were not. This fact so frightened some people in the West that President Sukarno felt it necessary to calm their fears by stating: "The Bandung Conference is not an Islamic Conference; it is not a meeting of Malayans nor one of Arabs, nor one of Indo-Aryan stock. It is not an exclusive club either, nor a bloc which seeks to oppose any other bloc. Rather it is a body of enlightened, tolerant opinion, which seeks to impress on the world that all men and all countries have their place under the sun."

But having said this, the President could not alter the basic fact that Bandung was a meeting of Asian and African countries, most of whom had fought or were still fighting the domination of imperialist powers. Thus, the resolutions were primarily concerned with issues of importance to those nations and their peoples. The Conference supported the right of the peoples in Tunisia, Morocco and Algeria to self-

26

determination; declared itself on the side of Indonesia with regard to the issue of New Guinea (West Irian) and supported Yemen in its fight to regain Aden. The Conference also acknowledged the right of the Arab countries to Palestine, and deplored the policies and practices of racial segregation and discrimination prevailing in large regions of Africa and elsewhere.

Colonialism was condemned, in all its manifestations as an evil which speedily should be brought to an end. Speaking on this issue, President Sukarno said: "For us colonialism is not something far and distant. We have known it in all its ruthlessness. We have seen the immense human wastage and poverty it causes, and the heritage it leaves behind when, eventually, it is driven out by the inevitable march of history."

We would gladly have remained in Bandung but because of our tight schedule we were forced to continue on our way. From Bandung the road led to Tjirebon (also called Cheribon), a small but colourful port on the northern coast of Java. When we arrived there, the narrow street was crowded. Women shoppers, some in Indonesian dress and others in frocks, were scurrying here and there in an attempt to finish their shopping before the bazaars closed. For in Javanese cities, as in France and Italy, there is an afternoon siesta lasting from noon until four-thirty or five o'clock. Unlike the women, the men were basking in the sunlight, smoking and chatting, completely at ease.

After seeing something of the town we decided to have lunch, and we entered a café that was quite clean and very crowded. Although we tried to get the attention of the waiter, we did not succeed. And so we sat, tantalized by the aroma of prawns, crabs and chicken being wafted our way from the nearby kitchen. Every minute we became hungrier and more impatient. Then I said to my husband: "I wonder what the word for waiter is in Indonesian, because we don't seem to be able to get him to notice us."

Apparently I was overheard, because a young Indonesian who was seated at the next table came over, and said politely:

"If you want the waiter, you must call him 'bung'. We refer to every man as bung regardless of his occupation."

"And what does bung mean?"

"It means elder brother."

"Elder brother," we repeated in unison, for having lived in India and Burma we were aware of the special significance of this term.

Who is more important or more respected than the elder brother? He is the sun around which the other brothers and sisters must revolve. Among Hindus it is he who lights the torch on the funeral pyre of his father. Among the Burmese Buddhists, it is the elder brother who is given the power to make all decisions when his father is away. In fact, throughout South-East Asia, to call a man brother, especially elder brother, is to bestow on him great esteem.

Pondering over this, we asked: "When did you start calling one another elder brother?"

"Soon after independence was declared," he explained. "It was President Sukarno's idea. He suggested that the term bung be used in order to emphasize the fraternity of the Indonesian people."

"And how was his idea received?"

"It spread as quickly as the fire we make to burn the straw after the paddy is harvested. You see, it was not difficult for us to accept such an idea. Except for the nobility, we have never looked down on a man because of his occupation."

"But do you really call all men bung?"

"Yes," he said emphatically. "And I will tell you something else, we even use this word for the head of our State. Although among outsiders he is known as President Sukarno, for us, since 1945, he has been Bung Karno."

Still smiling he said good-bye and after wishing us a good trip, "selamat djalan", he went back to his table. We waited a few moments and then with some hesitation, my husband called the waiter. "Bung," he said, "we would like some food."

The waiter nodded, surveying us with obvious approval. "I will be with you in a moment, Tuan," he replied, and soon we were eating a delicious dish made of shrimps and soy bean curds served with a hot, red sauce and a huge bowl of rice.

After lunch we began the long drive from Tjeribon to Semarang, following the coast line of the Java Sea. We had the road to ourselves. Once in a while we passed a bullock cart, the animals pulling the two-wheeled vehicle at a leisurely pace, while the driver dozed. What would India or Indonesia do without the bullock carts, those clumsy old-fashioned conveyances which carry so much of the produce? In Java the wooden wheels of the carts are taller than a man, so the cart itself seems to be perched high in the air. The bullocks are provided with soft shoes to protect their feet from the heat of the paved roads, and as they move in their dainty shoes, they look like over-weight ballet dancers.

Passing Tegal, a small fishing village, almost half-way to our destination, we decided to stop and enjoy the Javanese version of "the pause that refreshes"—coconut water. All along the way, coconut trees had guarded our route like military sentinels, and under the shade of many of them, the coconut sellers were sleeping. Finding one who was awake, we bargained for a large coconut. After setting a price, the vendor took a sharp knife and cut off the top of the coconut with one stroke. Then he handed it to Tuan, for in Asia the man is always served first. After drinking as much as we could of the refreshing water, we paid for the treat and started on our way again.

In the late afternoon we passed through Pekalongan, which is famous for its gay and light coloured batiks, and from there we drove to Semarang, a prosperous port city with a wealthy Chinese community.

At one time Semarang had been the capital of Mataram, the most powerful sultanate of Central and East Java. But early in the seventeenth century, the Sultan had bartered away his kingdom. Jealous of his rival, the Sultan of Banten, he called for help from the Dutch East India Company. The Company was only too glad to come to his aid because it enabled the Dutch to achieve a foothold in that part of Java. In return for military help, the Sultan paid the Dutch East India Company a certain amount of the rice produce cultivated throughout his sultanate, and he also agreed to prohibit his own subjects from growing coffee which eliminated competition with the Company's coffee plantations. Using this contract as a lever, the Dutch East India Company gradually broke the power of the Sultan of Mataram and gained complete control of his principality.

It was very hot and sticky in Semarang, so we decided not to spend the night there. Stopping at a small roadside stand, we asked the owner where we should go and she suggested a place called Salatiga. She told us that it is a beautiful town, nestled in the mountains like a jewel, and that we would find it cool and comfortable. Taking her advice we drove up into the mountains to Salatiga where we found a place to stay.

The hotel was built on the same pattern as the Transaera in Djakarta, for there was one main building and then small individual houses, consisting of a living-room and bedroom, for the guests. Hanging on the wall in the living-room of our bungalow was a portrait and when I

29

scrutinized it more carefully I realized that it was a copy of a Rembrandt. For a number of years, Rembrandt's most important commissions were from members of the Dutch East India Company, who became so wealthy in Indonesia that upon their return to Holland they could afford to be immortalized on canvas by this great artist. But because Rembrandt painted them, not as they wished to be, but as they really were, he soon lost his rich patrons and from then on was forced to live in dire poverty.

I was not sure if the copy of the portrait on our wall was that of Jan Pieterszoon Coen, fourth Governor-General of the Indies during the early seventeenth century, but it might have been. Handsome, haughty, his proud face filled with disdain, it could have been Coen, the Governor who broke the power of the Sultan of Mataram and who could write to the Board of Directors of the Dutch East India Company that under his management the Company was able to declare dividends of more than 150 per cent.

Just before going to bed, we took a walk along the narrow moonlit streets of Salatiga and heard the sweet call of the nightingale. Everywhere we walked there were bushes of poinsettias; like drops of blood the red flowers gleamed in the rays of the moon. In this setting it was easy to imagine Jan Pieterszoon Coen, dressed in black velvet with a white ruffled collar around his throat, wearing a fine plumed hat and declaring: "May not a man in Europe do what he likes with his cattle? Even so does the master here do with his men."

Chapter Three

EARLY THE NEXT MORNING when the dew on the trees glistened like diamonds, we left Salatiga. Although it was barely six o'clock, the crowd on the road was so dense that it might have been theatre time on Broadway or Sunday afternoon in Hyde Park. Java is the most heavily populated island in the world, and in some areas there are 1,000 persons to the square mile. But this is only noticeable in the morning, or when you are on a long automobile trip and in need of a comfort stop.

We threaded our way through an incredible amount of traffic. There were many betjaks. Although the drivers were poorly dressed, as they constitute a depressed group among the labourers, their appearance belied their independent spirit, for they imperiously assumed that the entire road belonged to them. They were challenged by the drivers of the dokars, who were neatly dressed in colourful sarongs, white shirts and black pitjis. The dokar is a small, horse-drawn cart that takes the place of a village bus and may be pulled by one or two horses. The harness is so heavily decorated with silver, and the horses so well groomed, it is hard to believe they are not on parade.

Bicycles were everywhere, hundreds of them, often with a boy pedalling and a girl seated behind, holding tightly to his waist. In Java one rarely sees a male on a bicycle without a female attached; in Bali never. In addition to the betjaks, dokars and bicycles there were lines of bullock carts plodding their way towards some destination. But all of this constituted only a small part of the traffic, for most of the people were walking.

The women were carrying heavy baskets of fruit or vegetables on their heads, their bare feet making clear imprints on the side of the road. They wore Indonesian dress, an ankle-length skirt, the "kain", which is made from batik material with bold, imaginative designs of deep blue on a rich brown background. Over the kain there is a "kebaja", a fitted jacket with long sleeves. In the cities the kebaja is made of imported cloth, printed with flowers; but in the country the women wear kebajas of hand-woven cloth, which though of rougher texture, are simpler and more artistic. Around their waist, partly concealed

31

by the kebaja they wear a broad belt of contrasting colour called a "stagen"; and for festive occasions a scarf of lace is draped over the right shoulder.

Those women who were going to work in the fields, protected their heads from the sun with straw hats. In each hat a knife for cutting the paddy was cleverly concealed at the top. Only the handle of the knife, like a decoration, could be seen. Many women carried babies, securely seated in a large shawl which was tied and looped over the shoulder. Thus the baby nestled against the mother's hip, comfortable and happy, while she was free to use her hands.

Weaving in and out of this mass of traffic, were men with shoulder poles, a device for carrying heavy loads which had its origin in China. The pole lies across the back of the man's neck and shoulders and is so balanced that there is an equal weight at both ends. Because of this, he is able to carry a great deal, but not without causing serious damage to his body. For as we came close to one of the older men we noticed that there were thick calluses on his shoulders and the back of his neck had been deformed from the constant pressure. But watching these men from a distance, walking so gracefully and quickly, dressed entirely in black, one would think they were not burdened at all. Suspended from their poles were sheaves of paddy, baskets of fruit, vegetables, stones, wood, charcoal, sulphur and even racks of painted sandals.

Other men, like butterflies among hard-working bees, were not carrying anything, but sauntered along, enjoying the beautiful morning. Near them were schoolchildren, almost all barefoot. Following the children were ducks, chickens, goats and dogs. So the scene was one of blending and contrasting colours, the bright clothes of the women; the brown eyes of the children; the red beaks of the ducks; the white hair of the goats; the black costumes of the porters, and as a backdrop to all of this, the vibrant green of the paddy fields.

To get through this traffic one needed skill and a sense of humour. Once in a while, a large truck would have to go by, and whereas in any other country, the truck driver would have engaged in a series of oaths, here he just laughed, while everyone else laughed with him. In Indonesia it is common to meet the most difficult situations with laughter; not with tears and certainly not with anger.

But though we were impressed by the panorama, which was charming and picturesque, devoid of the squalor which is so characteristic of rural India, still it was disquieting, for this is not the eighteenth but the twentieth century, and what we were seeing was an agrarian pattern that had been the same for hundreds of years. Women had always carried vegetables on their heads when they went to market; workers had used the shoulder pole from the time the Chinese first came to Indonesia; and the bullocks carts were as old as Indian civilization. Only the dokars, bicycles and betjaks were more modern, but even they hardly qualified as efficient means of transportation in our time.

Slowly the crowd dispersed and by ten o'clock the road once again belonged to us. There was not a sign of the excitement that had made the morning so interesting and hazardous. As we neared our next destination, my husband handed me a map and said: "Tell me how far we are from Solo."

There is something about a husband giving his wife a map which bodes ill for their relationship. Fearing the worst, I took the map and looked at it carefully. After a few moments, he repeated his request, and in a meek voice I said:

"Roger, there is no Solo on this map."

"That is impossible," he declared. "The bus that just passed us was marked Solo. You had better look again."

This time I studied the map more intensively—still no Solo—at which point my husband stopped the car, took the map away from me and said: "I will show you exactly where it is in one minute." At least five passed. The silence was deafening. Then he admitted defeat.

"There is a city marked Surakarta in the exact spot where Solo should be located," he said. "But you are quite right. There is no Solo." And so the spoils of victory belonged to me.

We came to Surakarta, as it is officially called, not knowing that it had two names. And from the moment we entered the city, which most of the inhabitants call Solo, we realized that it was quite different from the other towns we had seen. Most striking were the fashionably-dressed women, in their hand-tooled, high-heeled wooden shoes, decorated with gold figures, and their batiks, perfectly pleated with either nine or thirteen folds, draped so as to display to advantage the slender figure of the wearer.

It was the way they walked, slowly and gracefully, along the broad, tree-lined streets, carrying parasols to protect themselves from the sun, that gave an atmosphere of repose where there was no need to hurry. What was not accomplished today would be achieved tomorrow, even though tomorrow might never come.

We were easily seduced by this feeling of relaxation, and though we

33   C

had planned to continue, we decided to spend an extra day in Solo. Later, wandering about the city, we came to the palace or "kraton" as it is called. From here, for hundreds of years, the royalty moulded the life of the aristocracy, dictating the fashions, modes and morality. The ruler of Solo was known as "Sunan" or "Susuhunan", a Javanese title for supreme ruler.

We were fortunate in being allowed to enter the palace. Once we stepped through the huge doors, which were not arranged in a straight line lest evil spirits find their way inside, we were in a different world. The kraton is composed of a series of courtyards within courtyards, and many large open pavilions with decorated ceilings and floors of imported marble. Some of the pavilions are for receptions, others for performances of the gamelan orchestra and dance, and still others for discussions concerning matters of state. In one pavilion there was a bed, piled high with pillows and covered with satin. This was the bed used by the king on his wedding nights.

As we passed one of the pavilions, an elderly lady peered at us. She was wearing her batik without a kebaja, and it was draped over her breasts and under her arms like a strapless evening gown. I noticed that her lips were slightly discoloured from chewing betel. When I saw her, I greeted her in Indian fashion, putting my hands together in front of me and bowing slightly, as I had heard this was the custom in the court of Solo. She was pleased, for she came over and taking my hand, indicated that I should come with her.

We went a short distance and then she pointed to a pavilion where about forty girls were practising the famous Serimpi dance. They were all young and beautiful. Each one stood on a marble square of the enormous floor. The girls, like the elderly lady, also wore their kains wound under their arms so their bare shoulders gleamed in the light. As the gamelan played, each girl dipped gracefully, now to the right and now to the left. The dancers swayed like figures in a dream, so slowly that it was hardly dancing at all. There was no strength, no vigour, no excitement in this dance. It had become so polished that it ceased to be real.

Seated on a bamboo mat was the music master who was wearing traditional Javanese dress. His kris was tucked into his belt. In the old days this dagger-like weapon was worn by every male member of the royal family, for its absence indicated that the owner was in disgrace. The master's head-dress and sarong were made from the same fine Solo batik, while his jacket was of elegant imported broad-cloth.

34

Life in the palace had always been easy and luxurious based on the labour of the peasants who were forced to give a certain amount of produce to the Sunan and who also had to work without pay for the nobles of the court. They had to build the kratons and the temples; dig the canals and dams and defend the kingdom if it were attacked. The Javanese villagers used to say: "The court has its culture; but the people have their customs," indicating that between the kraton and the people there was a wide gulf.

The position of all the kings of Java, including the Sunans of Solo, was changed when the East India Company began to extend its hegemony. The relationship between the Company and the rulers was both subtle and complicated. At first, the Dutch needed the royalty to help them rule the people, but at the same time they were afraid that the regents would acquire too much power. This fear was expressed in a letter sent by the fourth Governor-General of the Netherland India, Jan Pietersz. Coen, to the directors of the Dutch East India Company in 1618.

"From various indications," he wrote, "it appears to be true not only that the kings of Banten and Djakarta have conspired to murder and plunder your Excellencies' goods, but that well-nigh all the kings of Java have contracted with each other to exterminate us at one blow."

But the "one blow" did not come. The kings were too jealous of one another to ally themselves in a group. In most cases, as in medieval Europe, a ruler had power only over one city or one small province. Not since the fall of the Madjapahit Empire, at the end of the fourteenth century, had the islands been unified, and the Dutch were not slow to take advantage of this.

They curbed the independence of the rulers by demanding the compulsory delivery of coffee at a price which was fixed by the Company. Then they forbade the sultans, on pain of being put in chains, to uproot any coffee bushes, for these were planted on Company land which the rulers had in their possession, only by virtue of the Company's good will. With this announcement, the regents had to accept the fact that the ownership of most of their land had passed into the hands of the Dutch East India Company.

In the nineteenth century, Herman Willem Daendels, who had been sent as Governor-General to the Indies by Napoleon, decided to clip the wings of the aristocrats so that they could never fly again. In his own words he wished "to preserve the authority of the native regents in the eyes of the ordinary Javanese", while at the same time making them, "completely subservient to the aims of government."

The brother and nephew of the Sultan of Mataram opposed this policy and so they were placed in stocks like common criminals of the lowest order, in the miserable dungeon of Fort Tjirebon. Daendels suggested to the Dutch Resident there, that although the Government could not openly condemn them to death, it, nevertheless, desired to hear of their being put out of the way.

At each period of history, the Sunans of Solo, enjoying their wealth and their women, accepted the position of being docile vassals to a foreign power. Thus, when Sir Stamford Raffles, the British Lieutenant-Governor of Java, from 1811 to 1816, visited Solo, he was greeted by the Sunan with expressions of friendship and given an ancestral kris belonging to the royal family. A treaty was signed in which the Sunan agreed to give up the proceeds of birds'-nests and teak forests in return for a fixed money payment.

When the British interregnum was over, and the Dutch returned, the Sunan of Solo supported them in their fight against Prince Diponegoro of Jogjakarta, who had raised the flag of rebellion and asked for the Sunan's co-operation. Afterwards, when the Liberator Prince was defeated, the Sunan complained bitterly that he was not sufficiently well rewarded by the Dutch for his treachery to Diponegoro.

The last ruler of Solo was a young man, placed on the throne by the Japanese during their occupation of the islands. He was completely subservient to the dictates of his Japanese masters, so that when independence was declared, the populace decided he should be deposed. Bands of republicans surrounded the kraton demanding his resignation. The Sunan, seeing the unruly crowds besieging his palace, remembered the words of President Sukarno and began shouting:

"I am one of you. There is no more royalty. We are all the same now. Just call me bung."

Taking him at his own evaluation, the people agreed to call him bung, and to be sure he was really one of them they deprived him of his former power and made the principality of Surakarta part and parcel of the Republic of Indonesia.

Today, the kraton of Solo is just a series of pavilions that are rarely used. Some members of the royal family and their entourage still live there, but the Sunan has no power and can only bask in the memories of reflected glory. Socially, however, the royalty is still important and a Solo family claiming kinship with the palace gains a certain mark of distinction. Such kinship is not rare, for most of the Sunans had many wives and concubines, assuring an abundance of aristocrats related to someone in the kraton.

When we left Solo we were on the last lap of our journey. The beauty and fertility of Java had held us spell-bound for four days; a striking combination of the sea and the mountains; of wild orchids and cultivated fields of sugar cane, tobacco, corn and mustard. In one day we had watched the entire life cycle of rice, from that moment when the farmer, with his bullocks, ploughs the wet land, until the time of harvesting, when the women cut the full-grown paddy, each one taking a single golden sheaf with her as a present for Dewi Sri, the Goddess of Fertility.

In the Indonesian language there are three words for rice. When it is growing in the field it is called "padi" (paddy); when the grains are removed from the stalk it is called "beras"; and when it has been cooked it is "nasi". Although corn is the major item in the diet of the mountain people, and in unfertile areas sago or tapioca must be used, for the majority of Indonesians, as for most Asians, rice and life are synonymous.

Having travelled from west to east a distance of more than eight hundred and fifty kilometres, now at last we were entering Surabaja, following the River Brantas, which led us into the city whose name is taken from two animals, for "sura" means shark and "buaja" means crocodile.

There was a time when the shark and the crocodile were quarrelling because each one wanted to rule the world. Finally it was decided that the crocodile should be king of the earth, including all the rivers, and the shark would be king of the water, including all the seas. But one day the crocodile saw the shark in a river and accused him of breaking the treaty. A fight began and the shark was defeated, after which the crocodile was the supreme monarch.

On the place where the shark and the crocodile fought, and where their uneasy compromise came into being, stands the city of Surabaja, whose emblem shows the shark and the crocodile facing one another, while superimposed is a replica of the Heroes' Monument, a tall column which was erected in November 1952, to commemorate those citizens of Surabaja who died fighting for Indonesian independence.

Chapter Four

I WAS AWAKENED early in the morning by the sound of a flute and as I listened to the haunting tune I was glad we were living away from the main thoroughfare, otherwise the lovely melody would have been lost amidst the noises of the city. But when we first came to Surabaja and I saw our little house and its unattractive location, I was very disappointed. It certainly did not resemble the elegant homes we had seen while driving through the residential section of the city. In the fashionable Darmo area the houses were substantial and imposing, like the Dutch who built them, and there were no shacks or stalls to spoil the appearance of the neighbourhood.

But our house was one of a series of white stucco bungalows that had been constructed by Airlangga University for its staff, and like other universities, its building fund for residential quarters was limited. The road going by was unpaved, and for a long time unnamed, and across the street was a large kampung which had mushroomed into existence on land belonging to the University. The kampung dwellers owned goats, chickens, ducks and pigeons, all of whom considered our lawn as home. And to serve the people living in the kampung, many food stalls had been opened.

The inhabitants on our side of the road were employed by the Airlangga University as lecturers or professors. We were a motley crew, Dutch, Yugoslav, German and American, gathered from many parts of the world, reflecting the changes that have occurred since the Second World War which tore people from their roots and sent them scurrying, like leaves blown by a fierce autumnal wind.

On one side of us, in an identical four-room house, lived a Yugoslav, who had a number of barking dogs and a magnificent collection of classical recordings. We forgave him the dogs because of the records. The only thing we knew about him was that he did not like Tito, and he was waiting for that glorious moment, when Yugoslavia, seeing the error of its political ways, would again become a kingdom. Then he would go home. But until this happened, he was spending his time, and how quickly it is spent when one is middle aged, teaching at the Fakultas Hukum or law college, one of the three colleges in Sura-

38

baja affiliated to the Airlangga University. The others are the Fakultas Kedokteran or medical college and the Fakultas Gigi or dental college. It took me a long time to grasp the fact that in Indonesia, unlike the States, the word "faculty" does not apply to the teaching staff but to the college itself.

On the other side of us, in a similar house, there was a Dutch doctor, a tall spare woman with sharply drawn features, no longer young but having the energy one associates with youth. She was extremely hard-working and in a brusque sort of way most charming. When we came, she was still the Professor of Medicine at the Fakultas Kedokteran and a colleague of my husband. I will always remember her bending over a heavy medical book; the lamp light making her grey hair seem like burnished gold, as it must have been when she was a medical student many years ago.

And so we lived next to one another, if not in friendship, at least in amity. Our houses were comfortable and there was something about the simple way we were living which reminded me of the time I had spent in Longview, Texas, during the last war. Even the dust from the road and the brilliant sunshine evoked memories of Texas, but the high mountains looming so near us, dispelled the illusion.

In our Surabaja house the sanitary arrangements were somewhat different from those in Longview. There we had an ordinary bath-room, but here we had a "kamar mandi" or room for bathing and a "kamar ketjil" which literally translated means the "little room". Both were outside, although connected to the house.

The kamar mandi had a device I had never seen before, a narrow, concrete cistern for storing water, known as a "djeding". During my first days in Surabaja, I assumed it was a bath tub. Then one morning, while having coffee with several Indonesian ladies, I learned better, when one of them said:

"I have just heard an unbelievable story. Someone told me that an Englishman, who is staying at the Oranje Hotel, took a bath in the djeding and then could not get out. He shouted and shouted until one of the clerks hearing him, came to the rescue. But as the Englishman was very fat and the clerk very thin, they had to wait until two others came, to extricate the poor man. Can you imagine anything funnier?"

I could imagine any number of things that were funnier, but I didn't comment. After that I bathed in true Indonesian fashion, sloshing myself with water from a small bucket. This method of getting clean is very unsatisfactory if you are alone, but with some help it can prove to be quite a jolly affair. Among Indonesian families it is not uncommon for a husband and wife to help one another, the husband throwing water on his wife and the wife reciprocating. When I learned this I felt the shock an Indian would experience because there a good wife would die before being seen nude by her husband. In fact an Indian lady often bathes in her sari to be sure her modesty is adequately protected.

Next to the kamar mandi was the kamar ketjil, which has two other names. By ordinary people it is called, quite frankly, a "kakus" or toilet, but in better society this is considered an impolite word, so it is often referred to as the "kamar kiri" or room on the left. This appellation which seems strange to an American or European is usually understood by an Asian, because there left is always associated with evil.

Thus, the Indonesian word "kiri" does not only mean left, but it also means, "unfavourable, unfortunate and unhappy." This same interpretation of the word is applicable in India and Burma. If you are at a dinner party in either of these countries, you must always pass the food with your right hand; to use the left implies a deliberate insult. And in India, where it is not uncommon to eat by hand, you may only use your right hand, never the left, which is considered unclean.

On the island of Bali, where Hindu influence is still strong, it is believed that all the evil, negative forces are ranged on the left, and all the good, positive forces are on the right. Since primitive times women, because of the menstrual flow, have been considered evil. For this reason the Balinese apply many restrictions to women who are menstruating, "for in addition to her physical handicap is added the powerful taboo of pollution (sebel) which then falls upon her; she is forbidden to go into the temple, into the kitchen or the granary, or to the well. She may not prepare food nor, of course, make offerings or participate at feasts, and the wife of a high priest may not even speak to her exalted husband."

What these taboos have meant to women was made vivid for me by a story told by one of my Indian friends. He said that the most tragic event in his childhood occurred when his mother was going through her period and therefore, as in Bali, could have nothing to do with cooking. As they were poor and had no servants, she called in a neighbour to prepare the rice. The neighbour put the rice on the stove and promised to return. But when the rice had finished cooking the neighbour did not come back and my friend's mother was afraid to touch it for fear that the rice would be polluted. So it continued to simmer.

When the husband came home for his evening meal, and started eating the rice he found it sticky and unpalatable. Without saying a word, he picked up the pot of rice and dumped it over his wife. As they had no facilities for bathing except in the river, she had to wait until morning before she could wash away the glutinous mass. During the long night her son sat and comforted her. This terrible experience was never forgotten by the child who witnessed it.

Because our kamar kiri and kamar mandi were outside of the house, they attracted an amazing amount of wild life. There were always lizards crawling along the walls, happily engaged in the pursuit of flies and mosquitoes. Cockroaches were also prevalent, especially during the rainy season. At other times there were small hard-shell crabs moving about here and there. Once in a while a "tokeh" joined the menagerie.

The tokeh is a large lizard, whose strange call can only be heard in the evening or at night. If he repeats his call an even number of times it is considered unlucky for the inhabitants of the household, but an odd number is propitious, five for happiness and seven for wealth. I used to hold my breath while counting, hoping the number would be five, but the tokeh rarely obliged.

In addition to these characters who lived in our bathroom permanently, there were occasional visits from frogs and field mice. But the only time I felt the situation had progressed beyond endurance was when a snake decided to invade the premises. Fortunately, Pappa saw him first and killed him with a heavy stick. Pappa, the husband of Siti and the father of Yanto, was our gardener and watchman, a gentle person who was completely dominated by his capable wife, Siti.

Siti was a remarkable woman in many ways. In addition to taking care of us, she had time to be a loving wife and a devoted mother. Siti's only son, a little boy named Yanto but whom we called Manis, the Indonesian word for sweet, was bright and cheerful and very spoiled. Siti kept him so scrubbed that I often wondered how his skin remained intact. When he went out to visit friends or relatives, everything about him was clean and polished, from his peaked cap to his small shoes.

Siti, although not handsome, had the type of face that artists like to draw. A strong face with high cheek bones and well-shaped features. Slender as a palm tree and supple as a bamboo, she never seemed to tire and rarely slept. Like most Javanese, she laughed easily, but had a temper that flared quickly. She was interested in everything, especially politics, and was a bitter opponent of polygamy. She was critical of her namesake, Sita, the heroine of the *Ramayana*, whom she considered too meek and mild, always bending to her husband's will.

Siti, who loved to talk, knew a great deal about the people in Surabaja, and did not hesitate to comment sharply about their foibles. One evening when I told her we were going to a dinner party at the home of a well-known physician, she remarked: "Anyone who works for him has to spend most of her time close to the ground." And having uttered this cryptic sentence, she turned and walked away.

When we arrived at the home of our host, many of the guests were already there. They were seated in the living-room, but conversation was desultory as the old-fashioned chairs had been placed in such a way that it was difficult to speak without shouting. At one end of the huge room there was a grand piano, and on it stood a bust of Ludwig van Beethoven. Hanging above him, in a golden frame, was a hunter in a bright red jacket, surrounded by a pack of dogs.

After a few moments, I noticed a pretty maidservant coming towards the room. Just as she was about to enter the doorway, she began to bend forward. She went down, down, down. I watched her in horrified silence. It was obvious to me that she was fainting and that the tray, laden with cakes and glasses of orange crush, would slip out of her hands. Finally, unable to restrain myself, I said to our hostess: "The maid looks ill. She is going to faint."

The hostess looked at me, and for the first time since we came to Indonesia, I felt quite chilly. No one else responded to my plea. On the contrary, everyone acted as though I had not spoken. When I looked again the maid was moving along the floor exactly like one of the hard-shell crabs in our *kamar mandi*. On her outstretched hand was the tray, quite intact. She served all the guests, and when she was finished, she backed towards the door from where she had made her entrance, still crawling like a crab. It was only after she left the drawing-room that she again assumed an upright position.

Later, when I described this scene to Siti she laughed, and then taking a tray and placing some dishes on it, she also went down, down, down and with surprising agility moved around the room at top speed. When I asked her where she had acquired such skill, she said that when she was a girl, she had gone to serve at the palace in Solo, and there all the servants were required to assume this position when waiting upon the royalty.

"But I hated it," she declared passionately. "That is the position for a slave, not for a free person."

And then she added with much feeling: "I don't even like to speak Javanese because it is too undemocratic. In Javanese, if I speak to someone who is my superior I must speak in high Javanese, but he speaks to me in low Javanese. But when I address Yanto, I use low Javanese and he answers in high Javanese. It is only when you are with a person of your exact social standing that you may use middle Javanese. I much prefer Bahasa Indonesia where everyone is spoken to as an equal." But though Siti resented Javanese, I noted that she taught it to Yanto, and whenever company came, he spoke to them, as any well-brought-up child should, in high Javanese.

In addition to Siti, Pappa and Yanto, our household included Sumiyati, the cook. She was a kind woman but lacking Siti's fire and personality, for her ways had been moulded during the Dutch period. She was an excellent cook, but rarely told me how much she spent at the bazaar. Once in a while, I would ask her about the purchases she made and this would entail a very detailed explanation.

"You see, Njonja," she would say, "everything is very expensive. This morning I bought all the things you wanted at the pasar, and in addition, when I saw some delicious avocadoes, I bought a few, knowing how much Tuan likes them. Then I remembered that we needed flour and salt, so I went to the store, because the flour and the salt in the bazaar are not of good quality."

Before I could say a word she continued: "On my way here, I met some boys and girls who were collecting funds for their organization because they are getting ready to celebrate Youth Day."

At this point, Siti, who had been listening attentively, interrupted to ask: "Do you know anything about Youth Day?" I shook my head. "Of course, you wouldn't know much about it," she said, "because you have just come to Indonesia. But for us, it is a very important day. Twenty-nine years ago, in 1928, many young people met in Djakarta. Some were from Java, others from different islands. They called themselves the Young Ambon group, or the Young Sumatra group or the Young Java group. But at this meeting they decided to form one organization and call it, Young Indonesia. They said—we are of the same people, the Indonesian people; we have the same fatherland, the Indonesian fatherland; and we have the same language, the Indonesian language. Therefore, we are all Indonesians, and not just different

43

groups from different islands. Ever since then we have thought of our-selves as Indonesians."

"And since independence," Sumiyati concluded, "we celebrate Youth Day on October twenty-sixth. So I gave the young people a donation of ten rupiahs, eight from you, one from Siti and one from me. They were very pleased. And finally, Njonja, before entering the house, the flower-seller stopped me and I bought some Gladiolas for you," and she thrust a huge bouquet into my hands.

Overwhelmed by this display, I started to leave the kitchen in what might have been described as a strategic retreat, when Sumiyati called me back, and smiling mischievously, said: "I am sure that you will be happy to learn that even though I made so many purchases and gave a donation for Youth Day, I only spent twenty-five more rupiahs than you gave me."

She said this with such aplomb that I burst into laughter, and de-cided then and there that we had engaged an extravagant cook. But I soon learned that spending more than you earn is a national charac-teristic. In the middle of the month almost every employer is asked by at least one of his workers for a "persekot" which is a special word for an advance on the next months' wages. Even the government, beset as it has been by financial stringency, is extravagant.

The Indonesians love life more than money. Like the impecunious grasshopper, they do not save, they do not worry, and they do not suffer; in Indonesia winter never comes. Though it is cool in July and August, it is not so cold that the grasshopper must regret his im-providence.

There are many factors which have contributed to the Indonesians' attitude that money is not expensive, and in this respect the difference between an Indonesian and an Indian is most striking. Thus, when an Indonesian, who lived across the road from us in the kampung, was fired, one of the Indian clerks working in the same shop, took him aside and said:

"I am so sorry you have lost your job, but if you listen to me you can get it back. All you have to do is go to the boss and say: 'Sahib, I am a poor man. I have four children to support. If you do not take me back how will we eat? I know you are generous and kind-hearted. So, Sahib, if you give me one more chance I will prove my worth!' If you say all of this and act as though you mean it, I am sure he will take you back.'

The Indonesian looked at him and began laughing. "You expect

44

me," he said, "to go and beg for this miserable job and, in addition, flatter that skinflint. Not me. In the first place, I don't have four children. I have seven. In the second place, whether I work or not, my children will eat because my wife is a nurse and earns more than I do. In the third place, I can always return to my village and till the land. And finally, if neither my wife nor I are employed, we will be kept going by the co-operative. So you can see, I have nothing to worry about, and the generous and kind-hearted Sahib can keep his job."

The clerk gave a heart-felt sigh, and then said: "I just can't understand you. If I were to lose my job, I would die."

The difference between the two men was not a personal one. They were both young, strong and hard-working; but what determined their different outlooks were the social and economic conditions which had moulded them. It was impossible for the Indonesian to realize the problems facing his Indian friend, who lived in a world of fear. Even in a land of plenty like Indonesia, he could not relax and enjoy himself for behind him like a shadow, was the knowledge of the hardships he would undergo if he ever returned to his homeland.

To obtain a job and hold it is the single most important factor in the life of an Indian, and for this reason he is prepared to cringe before his employer. He knows there are hundreds of jobless waiting to take his place. Most Indians support, not only their immediate families, but a father or mother and sisters or brothers. If he has no job, he cannot go back to the village and become a farmer. Unlike Indonesia, where the difference between the town and the village is minimal, in India to go back to the village is to return to the Middle Ages. But even if he were willing to do so, his caste might not permit it. A clerk digging in the dirt; soiling his hands; following the bullocks with a plough—impossible! He would starve first.

But for an Indonesian who has social mobility, who is willing to do almost any kind of work including manual labour, and who is not restricted by caste, life is not only simpler but happier.

From our windows we could watch the neighbours across the street. Some were very poor, such as the betjak drivers; others were better off because they worked in factories. Many were employed as nurses or technicians at the Rumah Sakit Umum Pusat, which is the central hospital attached to the Fakultas Kedokteran. Though hardship was a constant companion of the kampung dwellers, they seemed to be endowed with an ability to enjoy life; to savour each passing moment. Poverty which often breeds cruelty, meanness, slyness and brutality, did not change the basic warm and kindly nature of these people. There was no drunkenness. They rarely quarrelled, and they covered their children with a blanket of love that protected them from the harsher aspects of life.

So affectionate were they towards their children, that when they noticed the wife of one of the professors on our side of the street beating her three-year-old girl, they were shocked. After that, they referred to her as "Njonja Kegilaan,"—literally the half-mad woman. Children were their pride and joy. They had many, five, six, seven and sometimes eight or nine. Both parents shared in taking care of the little ones, but if a boy were naughty his father would call the mother to punish him. Usually, the naughty boy would be scolded and sometimes given a few slaps, but always by the mother. When I asked Siti why this was so, she said that among the Javanese there is a belief that if a son is punished by his father he will resent it, but will forgive his mother for anything she does.

Although the children in the kampung who were over ten were given many responsibilities, the younger ones were quite free. They wandered about like a band of happy warriors, playing when they wanted to play, eating when they wanted to eat, and sleeping when they felt like it. They appeared strong and healthy, but this was an illusion, for Indonesian children, until they reach the age of five, are often the victims of disease caused by inadequate nutrition, infection or lack of adequate medical care.

In Djakarta, infant mortality accounts for thirty-four per cent of the death rate, while the mortality rate for children under five years of age is sixty-six per cent. Although conditions in Surabaja are a trifle better, often we would notice in the kampung the flag that signified death, a white flag with a red cross, and then we would see a tiny bundle being carried away by a group of sorrowing men. The women wept at home, for in Muslim countries, only men may attend a funeral.

Just as we found the kampung dwellers interesting, so were we a constant source of amusement to them. The difference was that while our knowledge of their lives was superficial, they really knew all about us. They knew our strength and our weaknesses. One day I noticed a group laughing as one of the professors passed by.

"Why are you laughing?" I asked.

"Because he has 'mata kerandjang.'"

"But if he has something wrong with him you shouldn't laugh. By the way, what is mata kerandjang?"

At this question they simply howled with laughter. Then one of them said: "Mata kerandjang is a deadly disease, and you are quite right, Njonja, we really shouldn't laugh at the poor professor."

As I walked back into the house I thought about the phrase. I knew that "mata" meant eye, and "kerandjang", basket, but I couldn't quite connect the two words with any illness. That afternoon when our Indonesian teacher came, I asked him: "What is this illness, mata kerandjang? It can't be serious because when I asked my neighbours across the street about it, they began laughing."

He also started to laugh, and then he said: "It certainly isn't a fatal illness, but it can cause a great deal of trouble. As you know, 'mata' means eye and 'kerandjang' means basket, but the two together have a different connotation in Bahasa Indonesia. When we talk about mata kerandjang, we mean a man, who even though married is interested in other women, and therefore has eyes as big as baskets."

How did the people in the kampung know that the professor liked other women? I had met him often and he seemed to be so stern and puritanical that I couldn't imagine his looking at anyone but his equally stern and puritanical wife. But I was wrong, and the kampung dwellers were right, and this was not the only time that they proved so shrewd in judging the character of the professors and their wives.

Among our entourage was the wife of a German professor who laboured under the impression that her mere presence in Surabaja was a treat for the "natives", as she scornfully referred to the people living in the kampung. One night, hearing a radio being played rather loudly in the kampung, she became annoyed. So she walked across the street, entered the house where the radio was blaring forth, and declared:

"It is too late for a radio to be played. Turn it off."

As the speaker on the radio happened to be President Sukarno her ultimatum was not obeyed. So she turned off the radio herself. The result was not what she expected because the women began beating her. She was saved by her husband, who hearing her cries, came to the rescue and took his sobbing wife home.

In a matter of minutes after this incident occurred, the kampung dwellers called a meeting. Everyone was invited to discuss the incident, and everyone came, including the children. After much discussion it was decided to call in reporters and have the story published.

Someone from our side of the street, realizing the seriousness of the situation, telephoned the President of the University, who immediately appeared on the scene. With the tact and charm for which he is famous, he only briefly alluded to the fact that the people in the kampung were squatting on University land, and then reassured them that such an incident would not be allowed to happen again. In return he asked them not to give the story to the press as that would embarrass the University. After some rather mild arguments, they agreed to abide by the President's request.

The next morning when we were discussing the event, my husband remarked to the head-man of the kampung, who was quite elderly and wore a neat beard parted in the middle: "I am impressed with the fact that you called a meeting about the incident and that everyone was willing to abide by the decision."

To this the head-man replied: "Tuan, professor doctor, I am glad that you have noticed that we act together. It is part of our tradition. I come from Sumatra, and belong to a community known as the Bataks. Among us there is a proverb: 'The word of a single individual is the word of a fool; the word of the multitude is the word of the wise'."

Chapter Five

ONE EVENING, not long afterwards, Siti asked me if she could be excused for a few hours. As she was dressed in her best bastik and newest blouse, I realized that the request was perfunctory. "Where are you going?" I asked.

She hesitated a while and then said in an off-hand manner: "I am going into town. In fact," she added, "I want to see a visitor who has come to Surabaja."

"Who is this visitor?"

"Njonja Fatmawati Sukarno."

"Where will you see her?"

"In front of the residence of the Governor."

"Then I am coming too," and I quickly changed my clothes. We hired a betjak and soon we were near the Governor's residence. A huge crowd had gathered including thousands of schoolchildren and some of the most prominent women of Surabaja, dressed as though they were going to a formal reception.

A few minutes later an open car drove up, and in the car was a rather plump but pretty lady, standing and waving to the crowd. Tears were falling down her cheeks. As she passed by us there was a tremendous outburst:

"Go back to the palace, Ibu."

"Ibu, you must go back to the palace."

"Ibu, you are the first lady of the land."

As the cries grew louder, the lady in the car became noticeably disturbed. Many of the well-dressed ladies were weeping as they waved to her. The lady in the car, who was being addressed as Ibu, which means mother, was Njonja Fatmawati Sukarno.

"Why are they shouting like that?" I asked Siti.

"Because Ibu Fatmawati is no longer in favour with the President and she has had to move out of the Merdeka Palace and stay by herself, although her children are still living in the palace with the President."

"But, Siti, I thought you were an admirer of Sukarno. I don't see how you can come here. It is disrespectful to the President."

"Not at all," she replied indignantly. "All of the poor people here and even some of the rich admire Sukarno. But we do not like the fact that he has rejected Ibu Fatmawati for another wife; you don't know what it means to a woman when her husband takes another wife."

"Do you?"

"No, because it has never happened to me, but Sumiyati's husband took a young wife, and now she has to support herself and the children as he gives all his money to the new favourite. That is why Sumiyati always looks sad."

As the car drove away, one of my friends, the wife of an Indonesian doctor, noticed me and coming over said:

"There is going to be a meeting where Fatmawati will speak. If you are interested you may come with me."

Siti said she would go home, so my friend and I walked to the hall which was jammed with women. Here and there, sprinkled among them, were a few men.

The meeting was sponsored by an organization called the "East Java Body for Co-operation between Women and the Military". The chairman, Njonja Wijono, spoke first, saying that this conference had adopted a number of resolutions concerning the problem facing Ibu Fatmawati. As she read each one, there was tremendous applause, more than I ever heard at a public meeting in Indonesia.

The first resolution urged the government to give Njonja Fatmawati the right to attend state functions and ceremonies. The second begged Ibu Fatmawati to attend all meetings concerning women. And the third begged her to stay with her children in the palace in order to make sure that they were educated in a fitting manner.

After this, the Commander of the East Java Military Area; the Commander of the Surabaja Naval Base; the Governor of East Java, and the Mayor of the city, a physician and member of the Indonesian Communist Party, all welcomed Ibu Fatmawati to Surabaja.

When Fatmawati arose to reply, she was so moved that for a few moments she could not answer. Her face was drawn and her hair slightly dishevelled. After regaining control of her emotions she began speaking. My friend translated for me as Fatmawati spoke; some of it being lost in the audible sobs of the women in the audience. She said that it had been difficult for her to choose between duty and her feelings of pain and love. But she had been able to conquer her innermost feelings and follow her path of duty. "In this framework," she said, "I have been able to come to Surabaja and meet all of you face to face."

Brushing away her tears, she told the audience that she was very moved because so many people had come to see her, not only women but men, not only the rich but the poor, even labourers and betjak drivers. She felt that they were all sympathetic to her and that they hoped her life would soon be better. "I have the impression that you are all expecting happiness, peace and love for me." She in turn hoped that they too would enjoy peace and love.

As the tension in the hall increased she became more agitated. Finally, in a voice that was filled with emotion, she said that she hoped the Indonesian people could carry on the struggle for their ideals. And then she added: "I suffer when I see my people poor, not able to buy proper food and clothing. So I hope that all of you, poor as well as rich, will be united to overcome the present sufferings."

As we were leaving the hall, I said to my friend: "I am puzzled by what has taken place. Was this really an anti-Sukarno meeting under the pretence of giving sympathy and support to Fatmawati? Is she really so outstanding as to deserve all of these tributes?"

My friend smiled as she replied: "Fatmawati is not outstanding at all. She is a sweet simple woman, without pretensions, who has become a symbol of those women who have been rejected in favour of another wife. The fact that she is still married to the President puts her in the limelight and makes it possible for us to use her as a symbol and to rally people in favour of a law which would prohibit polygamy."

"And how does this affect the President?"

"Politically, he is not affected. Were he to come to Surabaja to-morrow, he would receive a tumultuous welcome. Even the ladies you saw in the audience would greet him. But socially he is somewhat vulnerable, for were he to bring his new wife with him, an epidemic of headaches would force all the ladies to stay at home. This is the way in which they would show their disapproval of his having taken another wife."

"But don't you think it surprising that Ibu Fatmawati can appear at a public meeting and be greeted by the head of the army and of the navy, the Governor and the Mayor, all of whom in one way or another, must owe allegiance to the President? I don't think this could happen any place else in the world."

"Perhaps, this is a unique situation. I suppose greeting the ex-wife of the President, while at the same time not using the meeting to berate the President, is unusual. But it is all part of our determination to ban polygamy. As you know, our women are not in purdah, they are not segregated, they are not second-class citizens. On the contrary, we have the same rights as men for they were guaranteed to us in the 1945 Constitution. In the entire Muslim world, we are the most forward politically, economically and socially. But until the institution of polygamy is banned by an act of parliament, we will not remain content."

"And how does the President feel about such a law?" I asked.

"He is very much in favour of it," she answered, her eyes twinkling. "Why, without his approval we couldn't get anywhere."

Later, thinking about our conversation, I recalled that the Prime Minister of India, Jawaharlal Nehru, had said he would apply two tests to judge the progress of any country about which he knew absolutely nothing. They were the amount of steel the country produced and the position of women. These two things, he declared, symbolized any country's progress.

In India, the position of women is paradoxical. Probably no other country has passed so many laws to protect women's interests, while at the same time doing so little to see that those laws are enforced. Even today, the dowry makes the marriage bed. The family of the girl must be prepared to pay a sizeable sum if she is to get married, particularly among the middle and upper class. That is why there is an old folk-saying: "He who has no son knows no happiness; while he who has no daughter has no cares." Marriages are arranged by parents, and afterwards if the woman is unhappy, there is no escape. Even though a Hindu divorce law has been enacted, the disapproval of a divorcee by the community is stronger than the power of legislation.

If an Indian couple are invited to dinner, the husband will often come by himself. After offering one of a hundred lame excuses, he will finally admit that his wife rarely accompanies him to social affairs. But in Indonesia, couples are always together, which is an indication of their relationship, one of companionship as well as love.

Speaking before an English audience, the wife of the first Indonesian Ambassador to England, Dr. Hurustiati Subandrio said:

"In Indonesia an ideal wife is considered to be someone who is a good friend in life to her husband. Married women in our country share full responsibility in the tasks and duties of matrimonial life with their husbands. This can be said of nearly all classes of the community, with perhaps, the exception of the princesses at Court, who are kept in a world of luxury and seclusion, far from the realities of life. Particularly the peasant and working classes give equal partnership to women and men. The harder the living conditions, the higher the status for women."

Such freedom has its roots in the history of the nation, for as Dr. Subandrio pointed out, "The original Indonesian mind, which was already imbued with a spirit of great tolerance through previous religions, such as Hinduism and Buddhism, accepted the conversion of Islam with indulgence—even towards women's desire for equal rights."

That status of women has also been determined by "adat" law, the law of the village which is based upon custom or tradition. Because this type of law evolved according to the needs and desires of the community, it was less strict and more flexible than formal Muslim law. In most villages, illegitimacy is not considered a crime. A mother who has a baby out of wedlock is not cast out by her community, nor is her child ostracized. Under adat law, the man who refuses to accept the responsibility of fatherhood is the one to be condemned.

Nor is prostitution looked upon with as much scorn as in other countries. When a prostitute marries, which is often the case, she is then accepted as a respectable member of the community. Rape is unknown. A man would not think of taking advantage of a woman. If she does not want him, he will find someone else. Love is very important in Indonesia. It occupies a great deal of everyone's time and thoughts. Unlike the West where business, politics and sports all come first—in Indonesia it is love.

Nevertheless, in the old days most marriages were arranged. The Indonesian women call these "compulsory marriages". Among the Javanese, who do not consider it courteous to ask a direct question or give a direct answer, the problem of arranging a marriage could only be touched on by inference. When a Javanese family hinted to their daughter that the young man who had just visited was a suitor, she would not comment. But later, when the family sat down to dinner, if the food was too salty to eat, then they knew that their daughter was pleased.

In Atjeh, the northern-most province of Sumatra, the custom of arranging marriages still prevails. The people of Atjeh declare that "never will a well find a bucket by itself". Among the Minangkabaus of Central Sumatra, the line of inheritance is through the mother and for this reason women occupy a privileged position. It is not uncommon for a girl to propose marriage to a boy, through an intermediary. One of our Javanese friends, who was working in Central

Sumatra, had four such proposals, which he reluctantly refused as he was happily married.

The Bataks have a ceremony called the "Martandang", which is a gathering of boys and girls in the house of one of the older members of the village. The young people have a chance to meet, and then a boy will often select the girl whom he would like to marry.

In Bali, it is not uncommon to have marriages by elopement. The young people run away with the knowledge and consent of both families. But as soon as the disappearance of the girl becomes known, her "enraged" father calls upon his neighbours to come and help him find his daughter. A search is organized. Although everyone knows where the young couple are hiding, they are not found. When they return to the village their wedding has to be legalized in the Hindu temple, and the groom must present a pig to the Brahman priest. After the pig is blessed, and cooked, it is distributed to the villagers in a ceremony which usually takes place three days after the marriage.

Although, in Bali, "marriage by request" is permitted, in the nearby island of Lombok, for a boy to ask the girl's father if he may marry his daughter, is considered bad taste. To such a request, the father would answer: "Our daughter is a human being, not an animal. We will not give her away as a present: but if she were to elope with someone— well, what could we do?"

In Sumatra and West Java the wedding ceremony is a combination of rites largely influenced by the Islamic religion. In Bali the wedding is of a modified Hindu type, but in Central and East Java the ceremony is a mixture of Buddhist, Hindu and Muslim rituals. We attended a royal wedding in the town of Solo. The bride was a princess, of about twenty years of age, a classic beauty with the sharply moulded features that Indonesians admire. Her husband worked as a pilot for the Garuda Indonesian Airways.

When we arrived at the place where the marriage was to be held, we noticed an open hall with bamboo pillars and a thatched roof. The pillars were decorated with yellow coconut leaves, stalks of sugar cane and sheaves of paddy. Two banana trees, complete with leaves and fruit had been planted near the front pillars. All of this was symbolic. The coconut leaves stood for happiness; the sugar cane for the "sweet" life the couple would enjoy; and the stalks of paddy for prosperity, since rice represents wealth in the eyes of the ordinary Indonesian.

The banana trees were equally symbolic, for these trees sprout easily and quickly. They represent the hope that the bridal couple will have many children. For such an occasion, only a special variety of banana tree can be used. It is known as "pisang radja", the royal banana, for at every wedding the bride and bridegroom are the king and queen.

Seated in the hall were the male guests, including our host, the Prince of Solo, a man nearing sixty with fine features, a neat beard and moustache, and continental manners. In the back of the hall, where the bridal love-seat decorated in white satin was placed, were the women. They were wearing the finest kains I had ever seen, a special pattern worn only for weddings. Their kebajas of imported lace were fastened with precious stones. Mingling with their French perfume, was the aroma of fresh flowers, with which they had decorated their hair. All of the women wore ear-rings, necklaces and pins of rubies, emeralds or diamonds.

Soon after we came, the groom, escorted by his family entered the main hall. There he signed the marriage contract under the watchful eyes of an Islamic teacher, and then paid the bride's father the dowry of five rupiahs, thus legalizing the marriage.

In the meantime, the princess was brought by her female relatives from the back of the hall. At the steps she waited for the groom. When he approached, she smiled, and then threw "sirih" leaves at him. But before the leaves left her hands he had thrown his first. There was an audible gasp among the aristocratic guests, for this meant that he would dominate her, even though she was a princess and he a mere pilot.

On the first step a raw egg had been placed. The bridegroom stepped on the egg and broke it, proving his masculinity. Then the bride washed his feet with perfumed water, as proof of her respect and loyalty. When this was over, the bride and groom walked to the bridal seat, hand in hand.

They were a resplendent couple. She was wearing a kain embroidered with gold, and a jewelled belt around her waist. Her hair was knotted at the nape of her neck and decorated with diamond ornaments and melati flowers, which hung down over her right shoulder. On her forehead, curls of hair had been shaped with dark paint. Her eyes were heavily made up and shone through her thick lashes.

The groom wore a tall, white, fez-shaped hat. Had he been a member of the royal family, the hat would have been black. His kain was tied at the waist where his jewelled kris hung, decorated like the bride's hair, with melati flowers.

After a few moments, the groom rose and then taking some rice grains poured them into the lap of his bride. She was careful to see that not a single grain spilled, because if this happened, it signified that she would not be content with the provisions that her husband could make for her.

Later the father of the bride, an exceedingly handsome man, sat on the floor and crossed his legs. His daughter sat on one knee and his son-in-law on the other. His wife then asked: "Which one is the heavier?" To which the father replied: "To me they are both the same."

If he had said this a half-century ago it would not have been true, for the position of women at that time was far inferior to that of men. The changes which took place in Indonesia during the last fifty years were, to a large extent, brought about by an aristocratic and talented young woman. She is remembered as Ibu Kartini and her birthday is celebrated as a national holiday.

Raden Adjing Kartini was born on April 21st, 1879, into a royal family of Central Java. At that time some of the members of the nobility were permitted to go abroad for study. They returned from Holland imbued with the ideas of the European humanists. They brought with them the bold slogans of the French revolution, "liberty, fraternity and equality", as well as the memorable concept of the American revolution that "all men are created equal". But in addition to desiring independence, this group was critical of the restrictive and feudal practices of Islam. Many of them had been influenced by the teachings of Mufti Sheikh Mohammed Adbuh, a brilliant Egyptian philosopher who felt that Islamic concepts had to be adapted to the scientific trend of Western thought. As she grew up, Ibu Kartini found herself spiritually allied to those who were opposed to the backward aspects of Islam.

Educated in a Dutch elementary school, Kartini longed to continue her studies. But due to the "pingit" tradition, which prohibited a young girl from going out unaccompanied, her family refused to allow her. For a number of years she studied alone, and then started a school for girls in her own home. She and her sister were the teachers. However, she felt that her education was not sufficient and she begged her parents and the Government to send her to a training school for teachers in Djakarta. Finally, after much hesitation, her parents gave their consent and she was granted a scholarship.

Before she was able to accept this offer, she received a proposal of marriage from a great and influential man, the Regent of Rembang. She accepted his proposal, not only because she knew that this decision would please her parents, but also because she felt that through his influence she would be able to continue her work in the field of education. She was never to regret this, as her husband understood and honoured her ideals.

Having married the Regent of Rembang in 1903, with his encouragement she opened another class for girls in her new home. One year later, at the age of twenty-five, Kartini died in childbirth, but in her few fleeting years she had laid the foundation for Indonesian girls, past puberty, to attend school away from home.

During her lifetime, Kartini corresponded with many prominent Dutch women who were her friends. In those letters, she poured out her heart. They were published after her death in a book entitled, *From Darkness to Light*. In most of the letters she explained in poignant terms her views on the relationship between the people of Indonesia and Holland.

Writing to her dear friend, Mrs. Abednanon, on October 21st, 1902, Kartini declared: "Civilization is not at all a kind of private property of whatever person happens to be in a civilized country. Real and pure civilization also exists in countries and nations which are mostly recognized by the white-skin nations as inferior."

Voicing the same sentiment in another letter, she wrote: "With heavy hearts, many Europeans here see how the Javanese, whom they regard as their inferiors, are slowly awakening, and at every turn a brown man comes up, who shows that he has just as good brains in his head, and just as good a heart in his body, as the white man. But we are going forward, and they cannot hold back the current of time——"

As the current of time moved forward the Indonesian women became more articulate. Their first association which was meant to strengthen their position as mothers and housewives, was called "Puteri Merdeka", the Independent Woman. It was established in 1912, at about the same time that the women of England were beginning their struggle for the right to vote. Members of the Puteri Merdeka pledged themselves to fight arranged marriages and polygamy. This organization was so successful that other women's groups sprang up. In 1928, all of the separate women's organizations joined together in Jogjakarta as the "Association of Indonesian Women".

During the Japanese occupation, women's organizations were banned and some of their leaders were executed. After Japan's defeat, when fighting took place between the Dutch and the Indonesians, women played a large role. The Sultan of Jogjakarta paid them a high tribute for he said that without their devotion and bravery, Indonesia would never have won its independence.

In 1946, the women's organizations met again, this time in Solo, to form the "Kongres Wanita Indonesia" whose aims are to urge and maintain social justice, to guarantee human rights, and to implement the independence of the Indonesian Republic.

In the ensuing years, Indonesian women have become doctors, lawyers, dentists and diplomats. But this is not the real criterion which determines the position of women, for as Dr. Hurustiati Subrandrio has said: "It is not what the most capable of our women has achieved that matters so much, but rather how the majority live and work."

Chapter Six

IT WAS THE TIME of heat and tension, the difficult month of October, when all living things were waiting for the rains, as an impatient lover awaits his sweetheart. If only the monsoon would break, everyone murmured. If only the rains were here, was the constant refrain. But the heat was unrelenting.

In the kampung even the children were listless, too overcome by the heat to be interested in playing. The vendors who came by called their wares in dull, heat-sodden voices, and the vegetables and fruits they had to sell were soggy and wilted. Only the gado-gado man was not affected, bellowing like a bull he announced his arrival, and so powerful and enthusiastic was his cry that the kampung seemed to reawaken, and the children followed him as though he were a pied piper.

"Come and buy my gado-gado, not biasa but istimewa," he would shout, thus explaining that his was not ordinary gado-gado but something exceptionally good, for in Indonesian, "biasa" is common but "istimewa" excellent. Gado-gado is a mixture of vegetables, covered with a thick, peanut sauce, which is both sweet and pungent, and served with a "krupuk", a sort of pancake or tortilla, made from dried prawns that have been pounded into flour, and then fried in deep fat.

The gado-gado vendor carried his own kitchen with him. On one side of his shoulder pole the gado-gado was kept warm by a charcoal fire. The charcoal was contained in a heavy, round iron pot. On the other side of his shoulder pole, he had an intricate contrivance which held plates, spoons, a jar of water for washing dishes, a towel for drying them, and a small cash drawer from which he made change. The kitchen weighed about seventy kilos, a hundred and fifty-four pounds, but he carried it with ease. And though he charged only one rupiah, he served each customer with such politeness that one might think he was the owner of the city's most exclusive café.

Once in a while, during this period of heat, we would hear the rhythmic sound of the "gendang", a drum covered with goatskin and beaten with the palm of the hand rather than with sticks. The gendang announced that a performance of the horse dance would take place. The children of the kampung adored it, and even the adults were amused. The dance involved two boys, a few musicians and the leader.

After a sufficiently large crowd collected, the leader would snap his long bull-whip and the dance would begin. One little boy, riding a narrow cardboard horse, which he put between his legs like a broom stick, would shake a rope of plaited hair in the face of the other child, who was also mounted on a cardboard steed. The dancer with the rope of hair, which resembled a horse's tail, would pursue the other child, never letting him get away, and constantly shaking the horse's tail in front of his eyes. The combination of the movement of the rope of hair, the music and the crack of the whip, would send the second dancer into a trance.

Prancing and neighing he would then become a horse. He would go down on his hands and knees and walk, gallop and trot. He would eat grass, drink water from a trough, and respond to the whip in the same manner as a real horse. As the music grew louder and faster he became more frenzied, and only after the music ended was the leader able to bring the child out of the trance. It was a cruel dance and I was always worried that the leader would be unable to undo the hypnotic spell cast upon the little boy.

During those days of endless heat, I seldom left the house unless it was necessary to go to one of the bazaars and then only in the late afternoon. Throughout Asia there are many types of bazaars; each one having its own particular fascination and its own peculiar charm. There are gold bazaars, food bazaars, animal bazaars and the bazaar of thieves where stolen goods can be bought. But none of the bazaars I had ever seen were as unusual as the stamp bazaar in Surabaja.

This was located at the entrance to the main post-office. Crowded near the doorway were many men and women, all seated behind wooden tables, in back of which were huge boards of stamps. As soon as a prospective customer appeared, the chorus began:

"Buy my stamps, my stamps are the best, mine are the cleanest, mine are the newest, mine are the cheapest."

As I was about to walk into the post-office, one of the vendors stopped me and said: "Do not go into the post-office. It is very hot in there. Here it is cool and pleasant. You won't have to stand in a long line and wait your turn. You can pick your stamps at leisure."

It was only then that I realized that the stamps being sold were neither old nor valuable nor from a distant country. They were just plain, ordinary Indonesian stamps.

Going over to one girl whose smile was irresistible, I pointed to the one rupiah stamps which bear a portrait of Indonesia's handsome President.

"I would like a dozen of these," I said, handing her twelve rupiahs. She tore off the stamps but refused to take the money.

"A dozen stamps will cost you thirty-six rupiahs."

"But that is impossible. The stamp is clearly marked one rupiah. You are charging me three times as much as I should pay."

"Njonja dear," she said, using the informal dear and the formal njonja. "How would I make any profit if I were to charge you the same rate as the post-office? You are paying for the luxury of my having done the work for you. I was here early in the morning, while you were probably still asleep—you foreign ladies stay in bed so late —surely, it is only fair for me to demand something for my labour."

"But three rupiahs for each stamp is too much," I complained, and with this sentence my fate was sealed, for I had revealed my willingness to bargain. As there was no escape now, I continued: "I will buy them for one rupiah and fifty sen each."

"I will sell them, just because I have taken a liking to you, for two rupiahs and fifty sen."

"I will not pay a sen more than one rupiah and fifty."

"Oh, Njonja, how can you be so hard hearted. At one rupiah fifty sen, I make practically nothing."

She looked at me with such pleading in her eyes that I wilted: "All right. Two rupiahs for each stamp."

Reluctantly she agreed. I bought the stamps and as I walked away, she said: "Njonja, you won't have any trouble mailing your letters with my stamps."

I could hear her laughter ringing in my ears, and I laughed too. But just at that moment, as I was walking away from the post-office, I felt something wet and slimy hit my face. I put my hand up, and to my surprise, wiped away some spit. It did not occur to me that this was deliberate until I heard someone say: "Go home where you belong, Belanda." As I looked up, I saw a boy on a bicycle pedalling away.

When I told my husband, that evening, what had happened he took the matter lightly, but the next morning driving into the shopping centre we saw signs painted on buildings everywhere, expressing the same sentiment. GO HOME, BELANDA; IRIAN BARAT BELONGS TO US: DUTCH EXPLOITERS GET OUT: DOWN WITH THE DUTCH IMPERIALISTS: RETURN IRIAN BARAT TO ITS RIGHTFUL OWNERS. On shops owned by

Dutch people the slogans were more insulting. Some windows had been smeared with tar and a few had been broken. As we drove around, I noticed that there were no Westerners on the streets. The angry looks we received indicated that those who saw us assumed we were Dutch.

That afternoon, going into Zangrandi's for ice-cream, we saw a sign displayed: WE DO NOT SERVE DUTCH. And when the waiter came over he asked if we were Dutch. When we told him we were not, he did not seem satisfied and served us in a surly manner. We were curious to know why an Italian place would put up such a sign, but perhaps Zangrandi felt he must be careful to fall into step, lest his business come under suspicion.

After this, similar signs appeared in other shops. Flags began blossoming in the windows of every commercial enterprise, Indian, Pakistani, Egyptian, Iranian, Turkish, German, English and American flags signified that the owner was not Dutch. Only the Chinese hesitated to call attention to the shops in their possession. However when we went to a Chinese restaurant for dinner the owner swooped down and asked: "Are you Dutch?"

We noticed that he was watching the door nervously, and when we turned around we saw almost a hundred betjak drivers scrutinizing us. My husband gave the owner his United Nations identification card. Taking it, the owner went to the window, waved the card, and shouted: "This man is working for the United Nations." This explanation failed to satisfy the drivers. Then the owner asked my husband his nationality. He replied: "American." When the crowd heard this, they laughed, and in a few moments melted away.

The next morning Siti told me: "All the servants have decided to stop working in Dutch homes, and so the fair ladies can do their own housework for a change."

"But what about our neighbour, the Dutch doctor?"

"Don't worry, she is an employee of the Fakultas Kedokteran and is a good woman."

"There must be other good Dutch people in Surabaja," I said, and it surprised me that Siti agreed.

"There probably are, but they live in the Darmo area and that alone is enough to make them hated."

"But why should living in the Darmo area cause hatred?"

"Because before independence, not a single Indonesian person was allowed to live in Darmo. It was Dutch, Dutch, Dutch. Even a wealthy Indonesian could not own a home in that section. It was just for them. And so, those Dutch living in Darmo today are still hated. You will see—not a single servant will stay in a Dutch house in Darmo."

"Not even if their wages are raised?"

"Not even if they were offered the same salary as Bung Karno."

I could hardly believe this would come to pass, but a few days later when our neighbour came over she was pale as a ghost.

"What is the matter, doctor? You look ill."

"I am not ill, but I am worried," she said. "In the houses of my friends, all the servants have left, even where there are sick people and babies. The Dutch in Surabaja are unable to buy food or medicine. The storekeepers are refusing to sell them anything. I have been able to purchase some commodities in this neighbourhood, but after all, I am only one person."

Urging her to sit down and rest for a moment, I said: "Let me make you a cup of coffee."

She agreed, and while we were waiting for the coffee, she said: "Oh, this stupid, blind Dutch Government. Doesn't it know what it is doing? For the sake of a jungle-covered island with a handful of primitive people, we will lose all of our lucrative trade in Indonesia. We will kill the goose that has been laying golden eggs ever since the beginning of the seventeenth century. Why can't we learn? After the last war, instead of granting Indonesia independence following the English pattern in India, we tried to subdue the country by force and failed. Now we are preparing to sever the economic ties between our countries.

"All the Dutch in Indonesia know this. That is why petitions are going to Holland, begging the Government to reconsider its decision, and allow the issue of West New Guinea to come before the United Nations. The Indonesians are only asking to have the question discussed. We are living in an age of negotiation, when countries must be willing to take such problems before an international body. But of course, it's partly your fault."

"Why?"

"Western New Guinea is supposedly an important military area in the over-all planning of SEATO, and Dulles has pressed the Dutch Government not to yield on this issue, although ostensibly the United States is a great friend of Indonesia. In addition, the Australians are dead set against the Indonesians because they fear that if Indonesia is given the western half of New Guineas, eventually the eastern half for which they hold responsibility, will be threatened. But regardless of who is influencing our Government, the fact remains that the people who will suffer first are the 50,000 Dutch citizens in Indonesia. They are doomed."

"But doesn't Irian Barat really belong to Indonesia?" I asked. "Geographically it is within the Archipelago."

"No," she replied emphatically. "The people of that island are Papuans and of Melanesian stock. They are entirely different, speaking a different language and having different customs. Why should they come under Indonesian domination and be Javanized? I think that West New Guinea should be under our protection for a certain length of time, or perhaps be made into a protectorate of the United Nations. And then, when the people are ready for independence, they should be given their freedom, that is freedom from us and from Indonesia as well."

"But are people ever ready for independence?" I asked.

"I think you were," she answered.

"Maybe we were, but at that time, the British didn't think so."

She laughed, and then added: "Regardless of the substance of the dispute, we should be prepared to negotiate."

That same night, at a dinner party, we heard the Indonesian side of the story. When I mentioned that my Dutch neighbour had said that Irian Barat should not belong to Indonesia because its people were of a different origin, and did not speak the same language, my host answered quite heatedly:

"That is nonsense. There are many different groups in Indonesia. That is why we say Bhinneka Tunngal Ika, Unity in Diversity. We are a nation of many ethnological groups, some so large they could be designated nations. And it is precisely this diversity which makes our country so dynamic. Our people speak hundreds of dialects. Surely, in view of this, Irian Barat belongs to us just as much as any other part of what was formerly the Netherlands Indies."

"But why did half of this island remain in Dutch hands after independence?" my husband asked.

The host pointed to one of his guests. "He can tell you as he was a member of the delegation that arranged for the transfer of sovereignty when the Dutch were finally forced to leave Indonesia."

The man he pointed to looked about thirty-five but must have been close to fifty. He said:

Handsome village women wearing Indonesian national dress on their
way to market in the early morning

(*Above*) A typical Javanese bullock cart

(*Right*) Child working in the rice fields

"During the Round Table Conference in the Hague, in 1949, we expected all of the territory known as the Netherlands Indies to be turned over to us. Of course this included Irian Barat. But much to our surprise, the Dutch delegation took the opposite point of view. At first we could not understand this, but later we were told that the Dutch representatives felt that they would never get Parliamentary approval of the transfer of power unless they could show that they had wrung some concessions from us which would retain for them a foothold in Asia, if only for military purposes.

"We were bitterly opposed to giving up Irian Barat, and for a time it looked as though the Round Table Conference would be wrecked on this issue. But the representative from the United States urged us to compromise, by accepting the status quo with the understanding that within a year from the date of transfer of sovereignty, the question of the political status of New Guinea would be determined through negotiations. And now, seven years have passed and Irian Barat is still under Dutch control."

"But not for much longer," our host declared. "This is the crucial year. If the United Nations refuses to take up the issue, we will find other ways of dealing with the problem."

Days passed and rumours multiplied. It was said that an influential section of the American State Department believed that the United States, instead of abstaining on the West Iranian issue, should vote with Indonesia. But there were counter rumours contradicting this; saying that such a move on the part of the United States was impossible because of commitments to Holland, one of the strongest links in the NATO chain.

Tension grew by leaps and bounds. In the middle of the month SOBSI (Sentral Organisasi Buruh Seluruh Indonesia), the most powerful federation of trade unions in Indonesia, issued a statement:

"The Indonesian people still attach great confidence in the United Nations for achieving a solution to the West Irian question despite the repeated disappointments.

"The struggle for regaining West Irian is a struggle for freeing the Indonesian people from Dutch colonialism in the economic, political and military field.

"To defend its economic and political position in Indonesia, the Dutch colonialists have used West Irian as a basis for launching aggression against the Republic.

"Therefore, the struggle for regaining West Irian cannot be separated from the Dutch economic domination in the territory of the Republic. In other words, the Dutch colonial circles can only retain their hold on West Irian by their economic power.

"Therefore, it is obvious that the struggle for regaining West Irian cannot be separated from the struggle to eliminate Dutch economic domination in Indonesia."

It was not surprising that SOBSI had issued such a political call, because in every country that has been under colonial domination, the main role of organized labour has been a political rather than an economic one. The struggle to win independence took precedence over all other activities.

The Indonesian trade union movement had its first tentative beginnings in the 1920s, as a result of the decline in the economy after World War I; the influence of the Russian Revolution and the subsequent formation of the Indonesian Communist Party (Partai Komunis Indonesia). These three events made it possible for the urban workers, in mining, transport and industry, to organize collectively and strike for better working conditions. The first major strike in Java was among the labourers who worked on the railroads.

However, urban labour represented only a fraction of the working class. The majority were agricultural workers employed on the huge plantations developed by the Dutch. Those plantations producing sugar, rubber, tea, coffee, coconuts, indigo and quinine, hired thousands of workers under semi-industrial conditions. Thus, a leading planter of tobacco in the nineteenth century, George Birnie, had "25,000 peasants under contract".

On the island of Java, where there was a surplus of labour, most of the plantation workers were employed on a part-time basis, except the overseers, the foremen and the skilled labourers, all of whom were Dutch or Eurasians. The unskilled Indonesians worked on the plantations during the season and eked out a living on their own small holdings the rest of the year.

On the island of Sumatra, where the largest plantations were concentrated, particularly rubber and tobacco, the situation was quite different. There, the shortage of labour was so acute that the plantation owners had to devise ways and means of luring workers to Sumatra. Using agents who promised high wages and excellent working conditions, thousands of Javanese and Chinese were persuaded to come there. But the honeyed words proved to be snares to trap the innocent.

The plantations were slave camps. Once a worker signed a contract, a penal sanction was invoked, according to which the labourer violating his contract was liable to punishment. A labourer running away from his plantation could be arrested by the police and, after undergoing a prison sentence, be forced to fulfil his contract to the end. The plantations were guarded day and night, and the overseers treated the men in the same cruel manner as the southern overseers treated the American Negro slaves before the Civil War. In fact, local Sumatran newspapers carried advertisements describing runaway labourers and offered rewards for their return.

In the 1920s an effort was made to help the plantation workers. Near Deli, on the east coast of Sumatra where the largest tobacco plantations were located, a number of strikes took place and as a result conditions were improved. Then, in November of 1926, an insurrection broke out on the west coast of Sumatra, led by the Communist Party which was supported, not only by the plantation workers, but by the entire population including many religious Muslim teachers such as Hadji Bahauddin. Unemployment, the rising cost of living and fear of losing the land, all combined to cause the insurrection.

Because of the fall in the price of rubber and the general deteriorating economic situation, the Sumatrans, who owned small pieces of land, were finding it more and more difficult to pay taxes. Once in arrears, the Government confiscated the land and then sold it to private Dutch owned estates at a nominal price. The prospect of becoming like the landless Javanese was one they could not and would not face, for everyone in Sumatra knew what suffering this entailed.

"The native land of Java has fallen into the hands of the commercial companies," a Sumatran writer declared, "owing to the fault of the Government. The native administration has acted as accessory in this. The people are reduced to misery; they no longer have any gardens, rice-fields, or clearings and can only work as coolies on the plantations. There is nothing left for their children and grandchildren but to sign on as contract coolies, and for their wives but to become prostitutes."

The Sumatran uprising, coupled with the unrest in Java, was the most serious threat that the Dutch Government in Batavia had faced. The Government acted quickly and decisively. Thousands of crack troops were sent to Sumatra. The insurrection was smashed. After this, the Communist Party was banned and more than a thousand people were exiled to Boven Digul, the infamous detention area in

New Guinea (Irian Barat). Despite this drastic move, the struggle continued. The number of arrests increased. In 1933, a mutiny broke out on board the Dutch man-of-war, *De Zeven Provincien*. But gradually, the movement for economic and political rights was stemmed, not only due to the repressive measures of the Government but also because of the great depression of the 1930s.

Thousands of Javanese, who had been working on the Sumatran plantations, were dismissed and sent back to Java empty handed. The Indonesian economy, dependent upon exports of raw materials, crumpled under the lack of a world market. A general deterioration in standards, which were already minimal, made it difficult for the people to continue their struggle against the Dutch.

Just as the economy began to improve in the early 1940s, the Japanese became masters of the islands. That their policy towards labour was cruel and dictated by their own interests is well known. Communists and trade union leaders had to work underground, and if caught, were killed. But at the same time, precisely because it coincided with their own needs, the Japanese encouraged the Indonesians to learn new trades and accept new responsibilities. Thus, though there had never been a skilled Indonesian worker on the railways during the entire Dutch régime, soon after the Japanese occupation, training classes started, and at the end of World War II Indonesian railwaymen were in charge of the entire system of rail transportation including administration.

Commenting on the Japanese occupation, Foreign Minister Dr. Subandrio has said: "It was a time of misery and torment, but out of it came some positive benefits. The people gained administrative experience; self-confidence and, perhaps, most important, political unity in the field of nationalism. The Dutch, for their own ends, had repressed the Nationalist Movement; the Japanese, for their own ends, encouraged it, at least by lip service. For their own purposes, they gave the people arms and encouraged military formations."

When the war ended and the Japanese capitulated, the Indonesians were far more experienced than they had been before. Because of this, they were able to organize effectively in determination to resist the return of the Dutch. In 1946, when armed conflict began, the Republican Government, which had shifted its capital from Djakarta to Jogjakarta, urged all political parties to participate in the struggle against the Dutch. The Communist Party was no longer banned. The Sentral Organisasi Buruh Seluruh Indonesia (SOBSI) was formed, appealing to workers on every island to support the new Government and to resist Dutch encroachment. At the same time, the Government passed legislation to improve the conditions of the working people.

After the final defeat of the Dutch in 1950, SOBSI continued to spearhead the fight for labour's rights, while at the same time maintaining its interest in political questions.

Towards the end of October, the Government launched a "West Irian Week". There were mass rallies and demonstrations urging the return of Irian Barat. We read in the newspaper that there would be a parade sponsored by SOBSI. That morning when I went shopping, the clerk said to me:

"I am glad you came in early today, as we will be closed all afternoon."

"Why are you closing? Today is not a holiday."

"No, but we are closing because of the parade. We are afraid that there might be trouble. As for you, you had better plan to stay behind closed doors."

"Don't be silly. We are going to see the parade."

"Oh, you really must not go," he said with genuine feeling. "It is not wise because you may be taken for Dutch."

"Even so, I am going."

"I wish you luck," he said. "All of your other neighbours will be hiding under the bed."

That afternoon as we left to go to the parade, we decided not to take the car and to go by betjak. When we asked the betjak driver, who lived across the road, to take us, he said: "I am also going to the parade, so you can have a free ride."

It was about four o'clock, when we arrived near the starting point. There were thousands of spectators lining the pavement on both sides of the street. Everyone was chatting and laughing. The atmosphere was not tense nor was there any sign of trouble. Instead we felt as though we had wandered into a group of happy holiday makers.

Many people spoke to us, asking where we were from and why we had decided to watch the parade. When we answered that we were interested in seeing what would take place, several of them remarked: "It is very good of you to come," as though they were welcoming us to a social gathering.

The spectators were neatly but poorly dressed. Among them I saw neighbours from the kampung with their children. There was nothing unusual about the audience. But when the parade began I was thunder-struck. What had I expected? Having seen trade union parades in many parts of the world, I thought the marchers would be in working clothes, carrying banners, singing songs and shouting slogans. What we saw was a parade that might have been composed of civil servants, teachers or clerks.

Every man taking part in the march wore an identical outfit, long white pants, a white shirt with long sleeves fastened with cuff links, and a brightly coloured tie. And never had I seen such white clothes, the whiteness gleamed in the sunshine, so bright, so filled with sunlight, that any soap manufacturer would have been proud to claim these clothes had been washed with his product.

The men carried small placards demanding the return of West Irian. No one sang or shouted. There was no music. The spectators watched without cheering. Only once was there applause, when a contingent of men belonging to West Irian marched past, and even then the applause was hesitant and delicate.

And then it was over. Two hours had passed, as group after group walked by. After all the warnings it seemed anti-climactic. I should have known that Indonesians are not given to emotional outbursts.

Without warning the monsoon began. As the cool water fell on the parched earth, every living thing was revived. Flowers began to bloom, the grass became greener, vendors shouted their wares with joy, bring-ing in from the countryside fresh, glowing vegetables and fruits, peas, beans, carrots, pineapples, mangasteens and huge yellow bananas.

Meanwhile, all of Indonesia anticipated the decision of the United Nations. The debate on the West Irian question was to open in the middle of November, and it loomed so important that the Government decided to send Foreign Minister Subandrio to present Indonesia's side of the case.

Nineteen Asian-African countries in the United Nations had put for-ward a request to the Secretary-General, to include the West Irian problem on the agenda of the Plenary Session of the Twelfth General Assembly. Two days prior to the commencement of the West Irian debate in the Political Committee of the UN, over a hundred thousand people crammed Banteng Square in Djakarta to hear President Sukarno declare: "Let us build our power and, if the Dutch in the UN will not meet our just demand, let us apply that power."

The debate in the Political Committee was heated. The Netherlands and Australia issued a joint statement, warning of the dangers inherent in Indonesia's desire to have West New Guinea. On the opposite side of the fence, the Bolivian Representative to the UN, G. Q. Galdo, said he was unable to appreciate the benefits that colonial domination had bestowed on West Irian.

"These people in our atomic age are still living in a completely primitive society," Ambassador Galdo told the members of the Committee. "The sacred mission of the colonial powers have suffered a fiasco in that part of the world. Because of that failure, West Irian should be returned to Indonesia which can lead their compatriots towards overcoming their backwardness."

Indonesia's Foreign Minister declared: "No nation with any sense of self respect can continue to allow its reasonable request for negotiations to be ignored, mainly because the other party thinks it can afford to take such an attitude on the basis of its present superiority in physical strength. This is a very dangerous attitude to assume and might lead to unforeseen and undesirable—even explosive—events in the international field."

On November 26th, the Resolution asking for negotiations between Indonesia and the Netherlands, and requesting the Secretary-General to use his good offices to facilitate such talks, was adopted in the Political Committee of the UN with forty-two votes in favour, twenty-eight against, and eleven abstentions. This favourable vote in the Political Committee heartened the Indonesians, until it was pointed out that this meant that the resolution would probably not obtain the two-thirds majority required in the Plenary Session of the General Assembly.

As the debate began in the Assembly, the Dutch businessmen in Djakarta became frantic, because in one of his speeches Foreign Minister Subandrio had pointed to the handwriting on the wall, when he said:

"How could outsiders, who cannot see with their own eyes the high ideals of the Indonesian people, accept the seriousness of this dispute, the sincerity of our nation in the struggle for West Irian, if according to the Dutch Prime Minister himself, the wealth obtained annually by the Netherlands from Indonesia, is still approximately 100 million guilders, and 50,000 Dutch citizens live in Indonesia in comfort."

This was the first official warning that if the United Nations refused to hear the West Irian issue there would be economic reprisals. A Dutch industrialist, who was a friend of ours, groaned:

"We are preparing to throw away 100 million guilders a year, for an island from which we cannot make a penny. In fact, we will have to pour money into West New Guinea. How can we defend a policy that is leading us to ruin?"

Attempting to explain the critical nature of the situation to the people in the Netherlands, a reporter in Djakarta, William L. Oltmans, arranged for a petition to be sent to the Dutch Parliament. This petition warned the legislators that serious repercussions were foreseen for the Dutch community in Indonesia, unless the Dutch Government agreed to negotiations. Four hundred members of the Dutch community, among them some eighteen Dutch professors at Indonesian Universities, signed the petition. But in vain. When the petition was publicized in Holland, Oltmans was labelled a traitor.

Indonesians waited impatiently for the final vote; the nation was poised for action. On November 29th, 1957, the resolution of the Political Committee was brought before the Plenary Session. The vote was forty-one in favour of the resolution; twenty-nine against, and eleven abstentions. It had not achieved the necessary two-thirds majority, although more than half of the total number of members had voted in favour. The delegate from the Philippines was so angry at having been pressured by the United States to vote against the resolution that he resigned his position at the United Nations.

After the vote was announced, Foreign Minister Subandrio said to the members of the General Assembly:

"Since the Assembly has failed to bring the two parties together, we have no other alternative but to take action outside the realm of the United Nations. We have duties towards the welfare and security of our people in Indonesia, and because an effort towards peace is shown impossible, we might have to take measures which will not improve our relations with the Dutch.

"Without any recommendation from the General Assembly, the Indonesian Government, as a sovereign government, and being responsible for the welfare of eighty-two millions of people, with a pure heart will now continue to carry the heavy responsibility until the welfare of the whole of Indonesia, including West Irian, is secured. I hope this is clear to everyone in the General Assembly."

The die was cast. There was no going back. Foreign Minister Subandrio returned home. At the Kamajoran International Airport in Djakarta, he was garlanded with flowers, while thousands of young people shouted: "Long live our determination to regain Irian Barat."

Chapter Seven

BEFORE THE GOVERNMENT was able to analyse the defeat it suffered in the United Nations or to crystallize plans for future activity in the West Irian campaign, an event occurred which overshadowed everything else. It happened on one of those nights when our electrical supply had failed and we could not listen to the radio. So, when we discussed going to Tretes, a lovely mountain resort about an hour's drive from Surabaja, we had no idea of what had taken place on the fateful night of November 30th, 1957.

It was not a pleasant morning, for clouds were gathering and rain was in the air. It looked as though the downpour might start before we left home. This was unusual, because the Indonesian monsoon is a gentle one and it rarely rains in the morning. But at the thought of spending even a few hours in Tretes, where we could swim in an open-air pool, surrounded by gigantic pipal trees and multi-coloured African daisies, we rejected the idea of spending Sunday at home.

As we drove out of the city it began to drizzle. The streets were deserted. The bazaars were empty. Just as we left the town, we were stopped by the Malang train. Just then, we saw in front of us a long line of vehicles that had been held up by a group of heavily armed soldiers, not traffic police but soldiers. They were signalling every car, bus and truck to pull over to the side of the road. Then the passengers and drivers were forced to alight, while the soldiers searched the vehicles and questioned the people. One of the soldiers curtly motioned us to stop, and although he saw the United Nations certificate pasted on the windshield, he insisted on seeing my husband's driving licence. Satisfied that all was in order, he allowed us to go ahead.

"What do you think this means? What is happening?" I asked my husband.

"It is a man hunt."

I could tell from intuition and from the way the soldiers behaved that his surmise was correct. The soldiers were surely trying to find someone who had committed a grave crime. But for whom they were looking or why, we did not know. All along the way the same scene was being re-enacted. We were stopped a number of times, and the

73

harshness with which we were questioned indicated the seriousness of the situation. Finally, being stopped by an officer who was less grim than the others, we asked him what had happened. He said: "Last night in Djakarta, there was an attempted assassination of President Sukarno."

Then in an unemotional voice which made the story even more macabre, he told us that the evening before, the President had gone to visit the Tjikini Elementary School in down-town Djakarta, where a fête was taking place. The President had a warm spot in his heart for the Tjikini School because two of his children, Guntur and Megawati, had been pupils there. Arriving amidst the cheers of the children, he saw many of the displays and watched several of the games.

At nine o'clock, surrounded by the happy and excited boys and girls, the President was walking towards his car, when a rifle shot was heard in the distance. A few seconds later five hand grenades exploded. Were it not for the President's quick-witted bodyguards, he would have been killed, but they formed a cordon around him, protecting him with their lives. Two of his escorts were killed instantly, Police Adjunct-Inspector Mohammed and Police Brigadier Achmad; while a third, the President's personal Adjunct, Major Sudarto, was seriously injured.

But the most terrible thing, the officer told us, was that so many children were killed. Nine had already died and hundreds were wounded. It was a miracle that the President had escaped injury for the grenades were lobbed at him from point-blank range.

When we heard the story we turned back, wondering who could have committed such a monstrous crime, involving the lives of innocent children. In a special bulletin, the *Bintang Timur* declared that this crime was inhuman because the would-be assassins knew that they were "hurling grenades at a festive place crowded with school-children".

Then this newspaper asked a question which was to be reiterated by every other journal throughout Indonesia. "Why should just Bung Karno have been made the target?" And the answer given was one with which the populace was in general agreement. The newspaper editorialized:

"There cannot be another reason than this: Bung Karno is the leader of the revolutionary struggle of the Indonesian people. Bung Karno is the main sponsor of the Pantja Sila and aligns anti-colonial forces which know of no compromise. So the terror against Bung

74

Karno was a political terror. A terror unleashed by groups who are against Sukarno."

Later, when the assassins were captured this analysis proved to be accurate. The men who had actually thrown the grenades were religious fanatics who had been convinced that President Sukarno was intent upon destroying the greatness of Islam. They were members of the Darul Islam, a terrorist political organization that wants an Islamic state, governed by Mohammedan law, and does not hesitate to kill people in order to further its programme.

Even before the Republic of Indonesia was formed, Sukarno had rejected the idea of Indonesia becoming a Muslim state. In the Five Principles, the Pantja Sila, which he enunciated just before the final defeat of the Japanese, Sukarno outlined his ideas concerning religion and the state:

"Not only should the people have belief in God," he declared, "but every Indonesian should believe in his own particular God. The Christians should worship God according to the teachings of Jesus Christ; Muslims according to the teachings of the Prophet Mohammed; Buddhists should discharge their religious rites according to their own books.

"But let us all have a belief in God. The Indonesian state shall be a state where every person can worship God in freedom. Let us observe, let us practise religion, whether Islam or Christianity, in a civilized way, the way of mutual respect."

It was this fifth principle in the Pantja Sila that won for Sukarno the undying enmity of the reactionary Muslims, including those who belonged to the Masjumi Party. This Party had been organized during the Japanese occupation. Its programme was sectarian and feudal and appealed to the businessmen in the towns, and the well-to-do peasants in the rural areas, who are called Hadjis, because many of them have amassed enough money to make the pilgrimage (hadj) to Mecca.

When the Masjumi came to power in 1947, after having defeated a left-wing coalition, it began an all-out offensive against the progressive forces as well as the communists. The tragedy that resulted from this policy was the Madiun Affair in 1948, in which many Indonesian soldiers, communist and non-communist were killed, precisely at the time when the Dutch were launching a major offensive against the Republican Government. Moreover, it was during this period that the Darul Islam came into being and gained a foothold in Java, giving credence to the rumour that the Masjumi was secretly supporting the Darul Islam and weakening national unity in order to make it easier for the Dutch to force the Republican Government into accepting a treaty which would give them economic hegemony over the Archipelago.

Within the Masjumi Party, there was such feeling against the policy being pursued by the leadership, that a breach developed between the moderate and reactionary elements. In 1952, the moderates formed another party, the Nahdatul Ulama (NU) composed of religious men and women friendly to Sukarno. Our cook, Sumiyati, was a member of the NU.

Throughout the years the Darul Islam shrank in importance but continued its terrorist activities in West Java. Because of the Darul Islam, traffic between Djakarta and Bandung is restricted to daylight hours. Anyone caught in the mountains after sunset, risks his life, for the bandits belonging to this organization swoop down upon the unsuspecting traveller, and not only take all of his possessions, but leave his dead body on the road as a warning to others.

One of our friends, working for the WHO, in Djakarta, went through an uncomfortable few hours when his lumbering station wagon developed a flat tyre in the hills. He, his wife and an Indonesian botanist were returning from Bandung when this happened. They had no spare, so the botanist volunteered to go to a nearby village where he would try to buy a new tyre.

While the doctor and his wife were waiting, a car drove by with some acquaintances who offered to take our friend's wife to Djakarta with them. This offer was gratefully accepted and she went off, leaving her husband with the stranded car. The sun was just beginning to set and a chill mountain wind was blowing. He waited uneasily but in less than an hour the botanist returned with a brand new tyre which he had been able to borrow. As tyres are so valuable and difficult to obtain in Indonesia, the owner of the shop would not sell the tyre, but was willing to lend it.

After jacking up the car and changing the tyre, they were ready to leave. When they got into the car they breathed a sigh of relief, but then they discovered that in all the excitement, the doctor's wife had taken the ignition key. What could they do? Again the Indonesian botanist agreed to go back to the village and get a mechanic to come and short-circuit the motor so that it would start without the key. Night had fallen. Our friend was alone once again. Suddenly a man appeared and flashed a light.

"Who are you?" he asked in Indonesian.

"I am a doctor with the World Health Organization of the United Nations. And who are you?"

"I am a member of the village militia. There is going to be fighting here tonight. As soon as you see a searchlight to the north, you will know a battle has begun between the Darul Islam and Government forces."

"Well, I am not worried now," the doctor said, "because you will be here to protect me, and I am glad to see that you are armed."

"When that searchlight goes on," the guard replied, "I am leaving for the nearest village where I can find shelter. I have no intention of being killed on this road."

"How about me?" the doctor asked.

"You will be all right. After all, you belong to the United Nations, so even the Darul Islam would not hurt you," he said laughing.

After that they waited in silence. As the moon rose slowly, hardly visible because of the clouds, the men kept their eyes on the northern hills. Within the hour a huge searchlight flashed the message. Seeing it the guard said: "Selamat djalan," and departed.

The doctor could hear shots being fired in the distance. After what seemed like a lifetime his Indonesian friend reappeared, bringing a reluctant mechanic with him, who fixed the car as quickly as possible. Thankfully, the two men resumed their journey to Djakarta.

Naturally, the Tjikini incident was linked to the West Irian crisis. The nationalist daily, *Suluh Indonesia*, like many other newspapers, discussed this aspect of the attempted murder of the President, declaring in its lead editorial:

"The fact that the Tjikini incident occurred one day after the voting on West Irian in the General Assembly, strengthens the belief that the destructive elements wanted to annihilate the Republic of Indonesia, or at least undermine the struggle of the Indonesian people. The Tjikini incident was a national event which deserves the attention of the whole community."

Because of this event, "the whole community" was galvanized into action. Without waiting for government sanction, labour unions began taking over Dutch enterprises. We were in Djakarta when just such a take-over occurred at the Transaera Hotel.

In the morning at about ten o'clock, a trade union leader came to the hotel; as usual well dressed and wearing the classic Indonesian pitji. He asked the waiters, the bearers, the cooks, the cleaners and the clerical staff to come outside. They all went out and sat on the grassy plot near the front entrance. Then he began speaking quietly without any oratorical flourishes.

First, he outlined the West Irian problem pointing out that the island was well known to all nationalist leaders because so many of them had been exiled there. He revealed that in 1927, he had been sent to Boven Digul, so he knew the island through personal experience.

"It is absolutely ridiculous," he declared, "to try to prove that the inhabitants of West Irian are so different that they cannot be considered part of the Indonesian nation. If racial measurements were applied to the existing nations of the world, America would have to return the control of its country to the Indians. The Soviet Union would be a kaleidoscopic pattern of racial fragments. In Britain there would be the Welsh, Cornish and Scottish nations, all separate and all engaged in quarrels over the 'national' boundaries. And Holland would have three distinct nations within her borders."

After this, he discussed Indonesia's defeat in the United Nations and the economic control that the Dutch still had over the country. "This control must be broken and we will do it by forcing the Government to nationalize every Dutch concern throughout the length and breadth of our land." He then came to the most difficult part of his speech because he had to convince the workers that if they took over the hotel they would not lose their jobs or any social security benefits. The older ones were frankly sceptical and asked many questions, but the young workers were enthusiastic. Finally, when every single person was in agreement, they rose and walked back into the hotel. They asked one of the bearers to knock on the door of the manager's office. When the manager appeared, they told him they were taking over the hotel.

The manager who was Dutch, smiled, agreed, and then shook hands with each member of the staff. When this was over, the workers went out again, and lowering the KLM pennant which had been fluttering in the breeze, they raised the red and white flag of Indonesia. The Transaera Hotel had become the Hotel Garuda, but not for long. Several months later when we returned to Djakarta we found that the name had been changed back to Transaera as there were too many Garuda Hotels in the city.

Similar take-overs, but on a far greater scale, were occurring throughout Indonesia. More than 336,000 workers on Dutch-owned estates staged a one-day strike and then began demanding that the estates be turned over to them. Many were, for the estate managers feared reprisals. But the most dramatic take-over was that of the ships belonging to the Royal Dutch Packet Shipping Lines, known throughout the world as KPM. One of the employees of the KPM, and a leader of the union, told newspaper reporters:

"After we proclaimed the KPM taken over by us, the workers, reports appeared in the newspapers that Dutch captains of KPM ships had received a cable from the KPM head office in the Netherlands to take their ships to the nearest foreign harbours. Upon reading these, we drew up a note containing the information and we took the notes to the ousted Dutch managers for their signatures. They signed. Thus, we had proof that the reports in the newspapers were true.

"This written confirmation of the Dutch managers was then sent by us to the Indonesian Army Chief-of-Staff, Major-General Harris Nasution. One day later, on January 5th, 1958, General Nasution decreed that all ships lying at anchor in Indonesian harbours were forbidden to leave.

"In the meantime, we heard of KPM ships escaping to Singapore and elsewhere, so we sent word to our Indonesian mates on all KPM ships at sea, especially those heading for Singapore, to have their ships returned to Indonesian harbours at any cost. Some of these KPM ships did not return to Indonesia until they were actually in sight of Singapore, and then they did so at the risk of the lives of our Indonesian mates, who were later decorated by the Indonesian Government for their courageous conduct."

At the same time, the Government forbade all planes belonging to the Royal Dutch Airlines from landing on or flying over Indonesian territory. This was a severe blow, because the KLM had enjoyed a virtual monopoly over international flights to Indonesia. No sooner was this announcement made than the vacuum created was filled by Air India, Quantas, TAI, SAS and BOAC. Although the take-over of Dutch enterprises was bemoaned in the European press, sympathy was not so overwhelming that companies from other countries hesitated to profit from Holland's loss.

The Garuda Indonesian Airways, for inland flights, broke its contract with the KLM; dismissed two hundred and eighty Dutch technicians, and established its complete independence. This airline had been set up at a moment of great historic importance, for on December 28th, 1949, the day after the transfer of sovereignty by the Dutch to the Republic of Indonesia, two DC-3 aircraft took off from the Kemajoran airfield in Djakarta to fly to Jogjakarta, which had been the seat of the Republic during the revolution. Coinciding with the international recognition of the new nation, the birth of an Indonesian airline became a fact.

GIA's first passenger was President Sukarno, who had given the airline its romantic name, for Garuda is the powerful, celestial bird of Hindu mythology which has the wings of an eagle, the arms of a man, the legs of a vulture and the speed of a jet propelled plane. And indeed, a bird as strong and swift as the Garuda is needed in Indonesia where the distance from Sabang in the west to Merauke in the east is comparable to the mileage from London to Montreal.

In Surabaja, as elsewhere in the country, the vice was tightening around the Dutch. Every Dutch-owned factory in the city was now controlled by the trade unions or the Government. Clamour for complete nationalization of Dutch enterprises became louder every day. The Government prohibited the publication of newspapers and periodicals in Dutch, which was a boon for us because the Dutch newspaper in Surabaja immediately changed to English. Telephone operators were asked to terminate the call if the people were conversing in Dutch. At the Fakultas Kedokteran, as well as all other academic institutions, lectures had to be given either in English or Bahasa Indonesia, as Dutch was forbidden. This proved difficult for many of the older professors who did not know English and were not fluent in Indonesian as their own mother tongue was Javanese.

Government instructions and regulations kept arriving from Djakarta with the suddenness of a streak of lightning and the ferocity of a thunder clap. However, the people remained calm and not a single Dutch person was harmed. But at the height of the West Irian campaign most Europeans in Surabaja hesitated to go out at night, except to the Simpang Club which has always been a haven for foreigners.

During the colonial days it was the most exclusive club in East Java, and except for a handful of the Javanese nobility and a few wealthy Chinese, people of colour were not permitted to enter the premises except as servants. During the Japanese occupation, the club was used as the headquarters of their dreaded secret police, and many nationalist leaders were executed in the courtyard.

Now, all had changed. Although still a private Dutch club, anyone with money and social position, regardless of race, could become a

(*Right*) A porter, dressed in spotless white and wearing a black *pitji*, takes his vegetables to market, carrying them on a shoulder pole which was introduced to Indonesia by the Chinese hundreds of years ago

(*Below*) A farmer ploughing his rice fields with bullocks

At the stamp bazaar

Sumiyati finishing a new *batik*

member. Even so most of our Indonesian friends were not members, nor did we join. However, we belonged to a film society that met on the premises. One evening, not long before Christmas we went there expecting to see a new film, but when we drove into the compound there were no other cars. As it was still early, we assumed that the others would be coming. A half an hour passed and no one showed up. Then, like an apparition, an elderly lady, dressed in black, who seemed to have evolved from space, came over to us and whispered:

"You had better go home. There will be no film tonight." Her voice was trembling.

"Why?"

"Because over there," and she pointed in the direction of the main club building, "they are making the revolution. And it is dangerous for people like you to be here."

"Making the revolution?"

"Yes, that is what they are doing. Listen. You can hear them."

We listened, but all we could hear was the faint sound of a piano.

"Please do go home," she entreated us, and then hobbled away, disappearing as mysteriously as she had come.

For a moment we could not decide what to do, but then my husband made up his mind: "In our eventful lives," he said to me, "we have seen many things, but we have never seen a revolution being made. And, if we don't see it this time, perhaps, we will never be given another opportunity. So, let us go over to the Club-house."

We walked across the compound, and for the first time entered the reception room of the Simpang Club. About a hundred and fifty neatly dressed boys and girls were jammed in the room, all talking and laughing. Some were drinking orange crush and a few were gathered near the piano where a waiter was playing a romantic Indonesian song, "The River Solo". There were several chess games in progress, with bystanders heatedly discussing each move.

Our appearance caused an abrupt halt to most of the activities and soon we were surrounded by a group who wanted to know who we were and where we were from. When they learned we were Americans, one of the older boys said, "I have been to San Franciso as I worked for the KPM. I was a steward. I loved the city. It is one of the most beautiful in the world."

They talked to us eagerly and when we asked them if they were making the revolution, they laughed: "No, we are not making the revolution," one of them said to us, "but we are taking over the Club.

From tomorrow on it will no longer be the Simpang Club but the Balai Pemuda, a centre for youth activities."

Although the elderly lady had not judged the situation at the Club with any accuracy, in one way her dire prediction proved to be correct, for soon after this incident, the Government issued a revolutionary decree which basically changed Indonesian life and economy. This decree declared that all Dutch financial interests were to be taken over by the Indonesian Government until such time when the Dutch would be willing and prepared to transfer sovereignty over West Irian to Indonesia. And further, that until this happened, all Dutch citizens living in Indonesia had to return to the Netherlands.

Chapter Eight

AND NOW a strange exodus began, for although the Government had decreed that all Dutch citizens living in Indonesia had to return to the Netherlands, the men and women, whom we saw in Surabaja, waiting for ships that would take them to Holland did not look like Dutch people. Almost without exception one would have assumed they were Indonesians. Perhaps because I was a stranger among them, neither Dutch nor Indonesian, and because they were lonely and frightened, some of them told me their stories. And as I listened, I wondered if there were ever an age when people were so buffeted by political events.

"I am going home this week," one of them told me, and in her voice I detected a note of pride, as though she had said something that had a special meaning that I should grasp.

"And where is your home?" I inquired, naïvely, failing to realize that this was the very question I was not supposed to ask.

"Home is Holland, of course. I am a Dutch citizen and I am leaving this country because the Government has decreed that all of us must go. My children and I are staying next door until we get the ship that will take us to Holland."

For several days I had noticed a middle-aged woman and her two children staying with our neighbour, the Dutch doctor. She was a typical country woman, in the Western sense of the word; not a villager, for in Indonesia the village women are noted for their grace. She was not graceful at all, but clumsy and awkward with large hands and feet, and the dress she wore only served to emphasize her heavy frame.

But what was most surprising was her face, which did not seem to belong to her body. It was small, oval shaped and delicate. Her features were well formed and her eyes were Indonesian eyes, deep brown, hidden under lashes as thick as velvet. She wore her long hair in Javanese style.

"And will your husband also go to Holland?" I asked.

"No," she replied. "He left me years ago and I obtained a divorce on grounds of desertion. He was a curious man, hard-working, good-natured, but with one serious flaw."

83

"And what was that?"

"He always sided with the Indonesians against his own people, the Dutch. I should explain that he wasn't pure Dutch, but like me, he belonged to the Eurasian community. His father was Dutch, and his mother Indonesian. And it was her influence that ruined him. Just because her own marriage was a failure, she came to hate all Dutch people, and instilled in her son that same feeling. He was so outspoken against the Dutch Government that he was almost jailed, and he could never get a job because everybody knew how he felt. Finally, in 1946, he volunteered to fight with the Indonesians for what he was pleased to call 'the freedom of his country'. Imagine, 'his country' and not only that, but a Christian fighting with infidels. So I told him I couldn't understand his wanting the riff-raff to run this place and turn it into a pig-sty. And then he declared I was nothing but a Belanda Hitam, a black Dutch. So I said, if that is the way you feel, then you can go and don't bother to come back. Off he went, and I never saw him again."

"But I do not understand how you were able to remain a Dutch citizen while living in Indonesia."

"After the revolution, Eurasians only became citizens of Indonesia if we asked for such citizenship, and very few asked, because we knew that as long as we remained Dutch citizens we could get financial aid from the Netherlands Government. Furthermore, we were given preference by Dutch firms having branches in Indonesia, and if we wanted we could go to Holland. But if we became Indonesian citizens, we were forced to throw ourselves on the mercy of the new Government, and I can assure you, the Government was not inclined to be merciful to us. Now I am so thankful for my Dutch citizenship, I just can't wait to go."

"Have you ever been to Holland?" I asked.

"No, I have never been out of East Java, but when I went to school we had to learn the name of every river and city in Holland. Why all of us know more about Holland than we ever knew about this country."

Just then, one of her children called, and as she turned to leave she added, as an afterthought: "I hope you don't have to stay here too long, this place is going from bad to worse."

Later when I went to try on a dress that was being made for me at the Java Modemagazyn, a shop that must have been elegant during the old days, one of the elderly sales ladies, whom I liked very much, took me by the hand and said:

"Very soon I will be bidding you good-bye, for I am going home."

This time I did not react as stupidly as I had before. I did not inquire what she meant by "going home". But as I watched her move slowly across the shop to call the dressmaker, I felt a tremendous sense of pity. When she returned, I asked: "Are you pleased to be going?"

"No," she answered. "I am afraid. What will I do there? I am nearing sixty-five and my husband is seventy. And here we have a nice life. We own a small house; we have three servants who have been working for us almost eighteen years, and we have friends. There, we will be all alone. And no one will hire me, I am too old, and too dark, which means we will have to exist on my husband's pension, and that will not stretch very far in a country like Holland where food and rent are expensive."

"Then why do you go?" the question was wrung from me against my will.

"Because I am Dutch. I am proud of being Dutch. I don't want to be taken for an Indonesian. I don't like the people who are running this country. I have no respect for any of them."

Then abruptly changing the subject, she asked: "Have you ever been in Holland?"

"Yes, once, for a short time."

"What is it like?"

This was a difficult question for me to answer. I had visited Holland just as the winter was beginning. It was cold and damp and grey. As we travelled across the country, we did not see the sun. The people, strong and square and hardy, were dressed in heavy woollen clothes. Just as there was no sun, there was no colour. Near the coast, the fog horns sounded incessantly, adding to the sadness and melancholy of the scene. But I didn't say this, because it would have been too unkind. So I muttered instead:

"It is a very fine country and the people are industrious," and then I stopped because it sounded foolish and inappropriate. She smiled, as if she had understood the hidden meaning of my words, and then she said quite simply:

"You believe I should stay here, don't you."

"I only believe that the transition will not be easy."

"You are quite right. It will not be easy."

We said good-bye and I returned home to find that the gas stove was out of order. I phoned the company and in a little while a young chap with light hair and a magnificent Van Dyke beard appeared on the scene. He had been to our home several times before but I had never had the opportunity of conversing with him. Now he said to me:

"I am really going to fix the stove this time, once and for all, because I won't be able to come again."

"Please don't tell me you are also going home."

"If you mean by going home, going to Holland, then the answer is no. I am a citizen of Austria, and I shall fly to Vienna. Thank heavens my father was Austrian. Had he been Dutch I would have had to go to Holland, and what would I find there?"

"What would you find there?" I asked, repeating his question.

"Trouble, nothing but trouble. Already over a hundred thousand Eurasians have gone to the Netherlands and they are treated like second-class citizens. Many of them have spent years in camps erected for the Indo-Europeans. They call us 'lippers', but they mean lepers."

"And how will you fare in Austria?" I asked him.

"Why there I will be a rare bird and with my plumage I should be the cock-of-the-walk."

"But aren't you sorry to leave Indonesia, with its beauty and its sunshine. Look," and I pointed a few feet away, "will you be able to have a banana tree in your own back yard when you are in Vienna?"

"I don't want a banana tree," he said laughing. "And I don't want to live in a little house like this next to a kampung. And I am not sorry to leave because this country is finished. They can't throw everybody out and expect to get along. They don't have enough technicians to keep the place running. So this is the time to go."

Everywhere we went we heard the same story, going home, time to leave, and mixed with this the constant display of fear occasioned by the knowledge that skin pigmentation would play a decisive role.

At the Cricket and Lawn Tennis Club I overheard one man say to another: "If you think from now until doomsday, you will never guess where I am going." The speaker, a slender man who looked as though he might be an Italian, was addressing a stocky individual with an intelligent face and a dark complexion.

"Where are you going?" the short man inquired.

"I am going to Australia. Right into the heart of the pure white kingdom. I will be the instrument of their contamination, but fortunately for me they were unable to detect the facts from my photograph. I looked a little dark for a Dutchman but not dark enough to give them the chills. So one week from today I will be in Melbourne, which only proves that my light complexion is more useful than your degree in engineering."

Another aspect of this complex problem was revealed to me a few days later at a luncheon party I attended. Seated next to me was a pretty blonde Dutch woman to whom I said: "You must be planning to go home soon."

She laughed. "I am at home. I belong here. My husband is Indonesian and I have accepted his country as my own."

I must have looked rather bewildered, for she added: "I know—it is just like being Alice-in-Wonderland—all the women you have met whom you thought to be Indonesian, are returning to Holland. And now that you are with a Dutch woman, you find she is staying here."

"Is this your own decision?"

"Of course. I have been living in Surabaja for more than twenty years. I met my husband while he was studying in Holland. I was also a student. We fell in love and decided to get married. But before he returned to Indonesia, he said to me: 'Although I love you very much and I want you to marry me, I think you should come to Indonesia for several months and stay with my parents. Then you will be able to tell whether you will be happy, for you will have to make many adjustments. Here in Holland I am a good-looking young student whom any girl might like to know. But there, I am a native, a man of colour, with whom no respectable Dutch girl would be seen in public.'

"I agreed to come to Surabaja and stay with his parents. Once here, it did not take me long to realize that when I married him I would enter a different world. Alone, I could do anything, go anywhere. When I was with him, there were restaurants that were closed to us, swimming pools that were closed to us and hotels that were closed to us. But it made no difference to me. I married him, and I have never, for one moment, regretted marrying an Indonesian."

"And have you children?"

"Of course. I am a typical Indonesian mother. I have five children."

"And are they happy here?"

"Certainly they are happy. They have some problems now. I had to take my youngest girl out of school because the children were calling her names, even though the teacher explained that her father was imprisoned by the Dutch for his activities at the time of the revolution. But the children are influenced by what they hear at home and during this campaign some ugly feelings have come to the surface."

"It is not easy," I said, and then remembered that I had used these very words before.

"No, but all of us have problems. And I think the most important factor in the lives of my children is that they do not have an inferiority complex about being Eurasian."

"That is because they have an intelligent mother."

"Not at all," she replied smiling. "And neither is it because they have an intelligent father. The answer is much simpler. It is because their father is Indonesian and their mother, Dutch. In such inter-marriages the children have few conflicts. But where the father is European and the mother Indonesian it is a different matter because if the father is not sympathetic to the Indonesian point of view his children will want to be like him. They will be ashamed of their mother and of her cultural background. Everything European becomes wonderful in their eyes, and everything Asian, ugly. These are the Eurasians who have been searching for a key which would open the door to the white world, a world which seemed to them to be concocted of happiness, wealth and security."

Dutchmen who came to Indonesia with the Dutch East India Company in the seventeenth century were pioneers, buccaneers and adventurers. They were not bound by the pious dictates of Calvinism. They were not, like their counterparts at home in Holland, sober and patient men, and such as believe that labour and industry is their duty towards God. They were gay, and free, and used to taking their pleasures at will, and nothing proved more pleasurable than being with Indonesian women.

As the years passed many such liaisons occurred, and marriages between high-placed Dutch men and Indonesian women became quite commonplace. If the man was influential, he could introduce his wife into his own social circle without fear of her being snubbed. In an English colony such behaviour would have been unthinkable. An English gentleman might take to his bed a "native" girl, but he would never bring her into the drawing-room. That is why Elliot Minto, the Governor-General of India, was shocked when he attended a state ball in Djakarta and saw many Indonesian women present at the gala affair. He was so upset by this experience that he wrote:

"There never is a dozen of women assembled in Europe without a few attractions among them. Here there was no difference, except for some varieties of ugliness and ordinariness of dress and manners.—The young ladies have learnt the European fashions of dress, still their carriage and manners are something like our own of an ordinary class. Their education is wholly neglected; or rather no means exist to provide for it. They are attended from their cradles by numerous slaves, by whom they are trained in helplessness and laziness; and from such companions and governesses you may conceive how much accomplishment or refinement in manners or opinions they are likely to acquire."

This society identified itself with Dutch aspirations; and was oblivious to the sufferings of the ordinary Indonesian people. But there were exceptions, and the most famous was a novelist of great ability, a Eurasian, E. Douwes Dekker, who wrote in Dutch under the Indonesian name Multatuli. Dekker's book *Max Havelaar* (1860) described the hardships of the Indonesian peasants who had to give a certain part of their produce to the Government. This novel shook the intellectuals of Holland in the same way Harriet Beecher Stowe's *Uncle Tom's Cabin* had shaken the abolitionists in the United States. So powerful was Dekker's book that the system of forced cultivation which prevailed in Indonesia, was abolished by the Dutch parliament.

But Multatuli was only one person, and most of his compatriots were occupied with social functions and hunting. It was not until the beginning of the twentieth century that Dutch women started coming to the Indies bringing an end to the Indische society. Then relations between the higher officials and Indonesian women became more clandestine. Dutch officials no longer married them, but kept them as concubines, "njais" as they were called. If there were children their fate depended on the father's attitude. If he wished to "recognize" them, he could do so, and then the children automatically became Dutch citizens. But if he refused the children had no status. "Sometimes professional 'recognizers', retired military officers, who for a fee of a couple of bottles of gin were willing to declare anyone as their offspring, did the job, and then the prized 'European' status was obtained."

However the governing class looked down on the sons and daughters of Eurasian parentage even after they were declared Dutch. The children of such a liaison were called "Indos", and their social position declined so that they were no longer welcome in the drawing-room. At the same time, the economic livelihood of this group became more precarious. The Indo-Europeans were faced with competition offered by newly arriving artisans and technicians from Holland. One Eurasian writer wryly observed that, "A Dutch man, who could not even get a job as a car washer in Holland, was able to obtain such a good position in the Indies that he soon owned a car, and then snubbing everyone else, declared himself to be another General Daendels."

The Eurasians were also confronted with the rise of educated Indonesians who were demanding government jobs, and whose demands were backed by the growing power of the nationalist movement. Confident of the loyalty of the Indo-Europeans, the Government was more interested in placating the intellectuals. So positions formerly held by Eurasians were given to Indonesians.

Caught in this vice, many Eurasians had to accept a standard of living that did not differ from that of a trained Indonesian. Yet, no matter how difficult the struggle, they resisted submerging their interests with those of their Indonesian colleagues. They were proud of their Dutch ancestry. They valued their European status. This proved to be their downfall, for when the Japanese occupied the Archipelago, the Indo-Europeans were singled out for particularly brutal treatment.

The occupation authorities immediately announced certain classifications for this community. If the father were Dutch it did not matter whether the mother was Indonesian or Eurasian, as this group was considered Dutch and placed in concentration camps. But if the father were Eurasian or Indonesian, regardless of whether the mother was European, Eurasian or Indonesian, those who renounced their European status, were considered as Indonesians.

The Japanese were especially cruel to the Eurasian women. One of my Eurasian friends told me that when the Japanese came she was already the mother of four children, but because she was young and pretty, she was imprisoned by the Japanese secret police along with her twelve-year-old daughter. She was badly handled but her only real fear was that the girl would also be mistreated. Fortunately, because her daughter looked small for her age, the Japanese did not molest her. When my friend told me the story, she said: "I cannot bear even to think of what happened. I try to pretend it was just a nightmare and that I awoke in time; or that it was a scene from a film that I was watching. But the reality remains and I carry a scar that will never heal."

After the surrender of the Japanese and the realization of independence, the Eurasians were forced to make another decision. A handful of courageous men declared: "Our destiny lies with the Indonesians." Among them was the grand-nephew of the writer Multatuli, who bore the same name as his uncle, E. F. E. Douwes Dekker. As early as 1912, Dekker organized a political party, the Nationale Indische Partij (National Indies Party), composed of Indo-Europeans, which advocated trying to breach the gap between the Eurasians and the Indonesians. The Party had as its motto, "The Indies for those who make their home there." But within a year the Indische Party was banned and Dekker, instead of being exiled, was allowed to go to Holland.

When Indonesia achieved sovereignty, Dekker abandoned Christianity; became a Muslim; joined the Masjumi Party; took an Indonesian name, Setiabudhi, meaning the "loyal one", and advised the Eurasian community: "Think Indonesian; become Indonesian; act Indonesian." But this advice was not heeded. Less than ten per cent of the Indo-Europeans opted for Indonesian citizenship. Most of them preferred either to migrate to the Netherlands or to remain as Dutch citizens in Indonesia, where they lived in splendid isolation until the West Irian campaign disrupted their lives once again.

Because of the Government decree ordering Dutch citizens to leave, nearly 40,000 prepared to return to Holland. Dutch technicians and specialists were told to go. The pressure against them was so great that even our friend and neighbour, the Dutch doctor, prepared to return to Holland. She represented that rare type of colonial servant who has no personal ambition. Her life was dedicated to her work. She was the only professor at the Fakultas Kedokteran who did not engage in private practice and she never enriched herself at the expense of the Indonesian community. But even so, her contract was not renewed.

The West Irian campaign had tremendous repercussions. After three hundred years of Dutch domination, Indonesia became the absolute master of its own destiny. Dutch personnel, Dutch economic and financial interests, even the Dutch language were swept away. But in taking such drastic action, the Government aroused the animosity of many countries abroad and some of its people at home, all of whom felt their interests threatened. They were not prepared to accept this situation passively. And so they set the stage for the next dramatic event.

Chapter Nine

THERE WAS HARDLY TIME to breathe; hardly time for the wind to caress the bamboo trees or for the country women to cut the ripened paddy, before the next climax shook the country like an eruption of a volcanic mountain. Early in February of 1958, a group of army officers, stationed in Padang, the capital of Central Sumatra, announced their intention to revolt unless the Government in Djakarta acceded to their demands. These were: the resignation of Prime Minister Djuanda and his entire cabinet; and the replacement of Djuanda by Mohammad Hatta, who was to be aided by the Sultan of Jogjakarta, Hamengku Buwono IX, famed for his heroism during the 1946–8 struggle against the Dutch.

The demands put forth by the rebels constituted bargaining points. What they really wanted was to engage in the time-honoured Sumatran practice of the "musjawarat", in which opposing forces come together and discuss the issues involved until everyone is unanimously agreed as to what procedure should be followed. Although President Sukarno is a great believer in the efficacy of this type of arbitration because it rules out the possibility of a majority dictating to an unwilling minority, this time he was adamant in his refusal to deal with the rebels and warned them to capitulate.

Once the rebels realized that there was no possibility of bargaining, a Lieutenant-Colonel by the name of Ahmad Hussein proclaimed a revolutionary government with full sovereignty over all of Indonesia. He also announced the formation of a new state, designating Sjafruddin Prawiranegara, as the Premier. Sjafruddin, who only ten years before had been the first Minister of Finance in the Republican Government, declared over the rebel radio station, located somewhere in Central Sumatra: "We are compelled to raise the banner of challenge against our own head of State. We have talked and talked. Now we must act."

What did all of this mean? What would happen to Indonesia? Whom did the rebels really represent? These were the questions we flung at one of our friends in Surabaja, a high-ranking military officer who had served with the Indonesian Army since its inception. Needless to say, he was far calmer than we were. At first, he just laughed and then with the nonchalance that seems to mark Indonesian behaviour in time of stress, he replied:

"It is a very complex picture, because so many factors are involved: trade, politics, international rivalries and personal ambitions. The motives behind the rebellion are difficult to unravel because they are related to the cold war as well as to our peculiar geographical structure and to the problems which arose as the result of our revolution.

"You must understand," he said, while skilfully rolling a cigarette with one hand, "that our revolutionary army was made up of inexperienced civilians. Boys of thirteen and fourteen served in the ranks; those who were fifteen or sixteen became lieutenants; young men of twenty found themselves commissioned as colonels. Abdul Harris Nasution, who is now our Chief-of-Staff, was one of the few old men who took part in the fighting. He was twenty-seven. It was a miracle that a handful of ragged boys using antiquated weapons captured from the Japanese were able to hold back powerful armed adversaries, such as the Gurkhas, the Sikhs and the Dutch.

"After this, the period of reconstruction seemed pretty tame. Some of the young men, who had tasted power, did not like the idea of becoming ordinary citizens again. They wanted to continue being leaders. And finding others who agreed with this point of view, they began forming small armed units. In Java, the organization which attracted these dissident elements was the Darul Islam. The situation became critical in 1952; the 426th Battalion of Central Java declared its intention of joining forces with the Darul Islam. This rebellion was easily crushed in five days. Generally, the Javanese did not support the insurgents but remained loyal to our national army. We have a saying that, 'the soldiers and the people are like fish and water.'"

"But what about the islands outside of Java?" my husband asked.

"There the situation has been somewhat different," our friend replied. "On the outer islands separatist movements developed mainly because the merchants did not want to pay taxes to the Central Government. In order to avoid such payment, a system of barter sprang up. Raw materials went from the islands—particularly Sumatra and Sulawesi—to Singapore, in return for finished products. As no money transaction was involved, the Government was deprived of revenue."

"And what did the Government do about this?"

"Very little except protest, as it did not have the power to implement its protests. The barter trade was extremely lucrative, and those who took part in it achieved wealth and then power. Naturally, army officers became involved in this type of smuggling. Gradually these officers and traders began to assume that they did not have any responsibility to the rest of the nation. But this effort to rebel would never have been possible were it not for foreign aid which was given in large measure to these dissident elements, and to the fact that they have been promised such aid in even larger amounts should the revolt in Sumatra succeed."

For the first time since he had been speaking, he became agitated and as he rolled his second cigarette his hand trembled and some tobacco fell on the floor. We could smell the pungent odour of the cloves which had been mixed with it. Quickly regaining his self control, he lit the cigarette and then continued, smiling and completely at ease.

"The leaders chosen for this adventure, who were considered adventurers, vagabonds, ne'er-do-wells, have suddenly become heroes, crusaders, champions of freedom. And who are these great men?" he asked, and now we could see that he was very angry for his eyes flashed and his hands were clenched. "They are traitors, who would betray our revolution and our Government for money. We know them well—Lubis, Hussein, Djambek and Simbolon. Lubis has been involved in a dozen unsavoury deals and he probably was the master-mind behind the attempt to murder President Sukarno at Tjikini.

"As for Simbolon, he is thoroughly unreliable as he was the leader of 426th Battalion which rebelled in 1952 and which we crushed. Defeated, Simbolon fled to the hills. Djambek is a coward. When he finds himself in difficulties, he will sacrifice his mother, his wife or his unborn child. And Hussein isn't worth discussing."

"What will be the outcome of all this?" we asked him.

With assurance he answered: "Why, of course, we will win. Not only do we have superior military strength, but many Sumatrans are with us. We can count on the loyalty of the workers in the oil fields and on the plantations. And the leadership of the rebels is bound to fall apart; interest in acquiring fame and more money will make them jealous of one another."

"But if the rebels receive aid from other countries, then what will happen?" my husband inquired.

"We will still win. Undoubtedly, the rebels will receive aid from abroad, but I do not think there will be any open intervention. The Dutch, who would like to see our country divided, will help the rebels in one way or another. Australia is hostile to us and friendly to them. Singapore is the nerve centre of the rebellion. The headquarters of the rebels is there, so they can expect aid, especially from the merchants in Singapore who have an important stake in the outcome. As for the United States," he shrugged his shoulders without finishing the sentence.

"But surely you do not think the United States will intervene."

"No, perhaps not. But we have not received the expressions of sympathy normally shown to a government when a rebellion occurs. On the contrary, your Secretary of State, Mr. Dulles, has already made it clear that our guided democracy is not to his liking. He told a press conference that he would prefer to see a government which is constitutional in Indonesia, suggesting that ours is unconstitutional."

"But his is not the only voice in the country," I said, "and I don't believe we will send arms to the rebels."

"You don't have to because there is always Taiwan," was his cryptic reply.

There was no answer to this, and so we sat quietly for a while each absorbed in his own thoughts. Then while we were having coffee, I asked him if he might be leaving Surabaja for the front.

"I hope so," he replied.

"Before you go, we would like to give you a 'selamatan'."

"That would be splendid," he replied.

About a week later he telephoned and told me he would be leaving very soon, so we set a date, and then I invited as many people as we could cram into our tiny house. We had a real selamatan, for we served the two dishes that are indispensable at such a feast; "soto", a spiced soup made from chicken, and "nasi kuning", rice tinted with saffron and served with shredded coconut.

After dinner, which had lasted for more than an hour, talk veered to the latest events taking place in Sumatra.

"Do you know what has surprised the rebels?" our military friend asked.

"No, what?"

"The fact that we are really going to fight."

"But this decision should have come as no surprise," I said. "In our country, when the southern rebels fired on Fort Sumter, they knew they were provoking a civil war and that the northern forces would fight."

"Ah, but your history is quite different. You are all hot-heads," one of the other guests, the handsome doctor from middle Java who had received so many proposals of marriage during his seven-year tour of duty in Sumatra, remarked. "We have a long tradition of resisting bloodshed. We don't like to fight. We like to negotiate. In the seventeenth century when the Madurese, who are our next-door neighbours, took up arms against the king of Surabaja, the king didn't fight. He sent emissaries to the island of Madura with power to negotiate. These emissaries talked with the Madurese, and finally persuaded them to agree to a compromise. A new Madurese chief was appointed and he was presented with a kris by the representatives of Surabaja's king. And so, of course, there was no war. The old chief who started all the trouble was forgiven, just the way we will forgive Simbolon and Hussein and the others after we have trounced them."

"Perhaps," someone suggested, "we will be able to settle this revolt without bloodshed."

"No," our military friend said emphatically. "Not this time. Such a possibility does not exist. We have a saying that we will not use our soldiers to fight brother soldiers, but now we must abandon this idea. Otherwise our country will be divided like Korea and Viet Nam. We are a unitary state and will remain one but only by putting down this counter-revolution."

Not long after the selamatan, we went to see a couple who lived near us and who were from Padang, where the heart of the Sumatran rebellion was centred. We were surprised to see how tired and upset they looked. They told us that they had not heard from their family in Padang for a few weeks and did not know whether they were safe.

"What do you think about the situation there?" I asked.

"Perhaps I shouldn't say so, but we Sumatrans are tired of the despotic rule of Djakarta," the husband answered, his face turning livid with anger. "We have suffered enough under their control. Although Sumatra is responsible for over seventy per cent of Indonesia's export revenue, we receive little in return. Our roads, our schools and our hospitals are in shameful condition. The money we earn, instead of being used to improve Sumatra, goes into the pockets of corrupt officials in Djakarta, so they can drive around in big American cars."

"But we have heard that the leadership of the rebels is also corrupt. How about Lubis?"

"Lubis does not have a good reputation, but he is not as bad as some people would have you believe. His character has been smeared by friends and followers of the President. But granting that Lubis is not entirely honest, one cannot say that about Sjafruddin Prawiranegara.

Since the very beginning, he has been in the forefront of the struggle for Indonesian independence. Were it not for Sjafruddin, Sumatra would have fallen to the Dutch in 1948. There were many Sumatrans, at that time, who did not favour the revolution because of its left leadership. Then Sukarno sent Sjafruddin to Bukit Tinggi, the capital of Sumatra, and he succeeded in convincing them that they should support the Republic. Because he was a Sumatran and a deeply religious Muslim, Sjafruddin was trusted. It was Sjafruddin who secured Sumatra for Indonesia."

"But why has he joined the rebels?"

"Because he is no longer able to agree with the President who has been captured by the communists. Sjafruddin is bitterly opposed to them. He is one of the founders of the Masjumi Party and the leader of the group within the party known as the religious socialists. The religious socialists believe in private initiative and private property but also in a programme of social justice for the people, especially the poor people. They are opposed to the Marxist socialists, that is the communists, and they fear the growing threat of communism. That is why Sjafruddin broke with the President and is leading the rebellion."

"But can the rebels win?"

"It all depends," he replied.

"On Allah?"

"On the will of Allah, of course. But at the human level it depends on whether this just cause will be supported by Mohammed Hatta."

So once again, Mohammed Hatta had become a pivotal figure. When we arrived in Indonesia his star had waned, but for many years he had been a figure of great political importance. Born in Bukit Tinggi, in 1902, of a high-placed family, as a young man he became involved in the Sumatran Youth Movement. Then in 1922, he went to Holland where he studied law at Rotterdam and became acquainted with a number of intellectuals who were active in promoting Indonesian independence.

In Holland, Indonesians were allowed to form organizations and edit journals that were anti-Dutch. Moreover, many Dutch students, intellectuals and trade union leaders gave them moral encouragement and financial support. While in Rotterdam, Hatta joined the Indonesian Association, and edited its magazine. In 1927 he attended the Brussels Congress of the League Against World Imperialism, an organization which numbered among its members Jawaharlal Nehru and Ho Chi minh.

G

While he was still in Europe, Hatta was influenced by the emergence of national socialism in Germany and later, the programme he helped formulate for the Masjumi Party was imbued with this ideology. In 1932 he visited Japan and then returned to Java. Early in 1934 he was arrested and exiled to the Tanah Merah concentration camp at Boven Digul. Freed by the Japanese in 1942, Hatta became the first Vice-President of Indonesia.

Although he had worked for independence, Hatta was basically an extreme conservative, and as he watched the revolutionary forces becoming bolder he feared a strong left. Therefore as a counter balance, he pursued a policy of appeasing Dutch interests. Thus, in his capacity as Prime Minister, he approved the decisions taken at the Round Table Conference at the Hague in 1949, which restored to Holland broad avenues of economic power over Indonesia, such as rights, concessions and licences for the operation of existing and new enterprises and estates. Furthermore, the Indonesian Government was forced to take over the debts of the Netherlands East Indies Government, which amounted to more than a billion dollars, and which, in effect, meant that the Indonesians were paying for the Dutch military attack which had been launched against them.

The reaction to these provisions was bitter and Hatta was dubbed a "kaki tangan nica"—a tool of the Dutch. The Agreement was unilaterally abrogated in 1956. As the years passed, Hatta also opposed Sukarno's policy of strict neutrality in the cold war. He wanted Indonesia to be aligned with the SEATO powers. Because of his orientation on national and international affairs he was now considered the one man who could be the ideological leader of the rebellion. The rebels waited for a sign that he was with them.

But unlike the Sultan of Jogjakarta, who was so furious when the press attempted to portray him as a pro-rebel that he took the first plane home from the United States to pledge his support to President Sukarno, Hatta did nothing. He did not give his blessing to the rebel cause, nor did he condemn it. He waited. But the country did not wait.

Everywhere there was intense military activity. Martial law was invoked. Curfews were declared. Long lines of trucks could be seen. The roads were clogged with jeeps, tanks and artillery. In the villages, boys and girls carrying bamboo poles, marched like soldiers. Everyone knew that an attack on Sumatra was pending. Nerves were on edge. People were excitable as the tension increased. Amidst all of this, my husband was invited to Singapore to give a lecture on tranquillizers.

Flying out of Surabaja, the window blinds of the plane were drawn so that one could not see the take-off. When we left Djakarta, the situation was more serious. The hostess explained that due to military restrictions, no planes were allowed to fly over or near Sumatra, and in order to comply with this ruling, the plane had to make a detour, adding six hundred miles to the flight between Djakarta and Singapore, nearly doubling the usual time required. The passengers, mainly Australians, grumbled audibly but there was nothing to be done.

As we flew, I remembered our first trip to Indonesia, when we had seen Sumatra lying below us like a glittering emerald, an island of mountains and magnificent lakes. Sumatra, thirteen times the size of Holland, the fifth largest island in the world, is famous for its natural wealth. As early as the seventeenth century, it was described by an Englishman as: "An island among the Javas, from whence cometh diamants. And the king hath a mass of earth which is golde; it groweth in the middle of a river; and when the king doth lacke golde, they cut part of the earth and melt it, whereof cometh golde."

The people of Sumatra, of whom there are many ethnological groups, such as the Lampungs in the south, the Minangkabaus in the west, the Bataks in the north-central region, and the Atjehnese in the extreme north, have varied traditions.

The Atjehnese, who are staunch Muslims, are the most independent people of Sumatra. The war between them and the Dutch lasted for forty years, from 1873 until 1913. In 1904, the Dutch were able to depose the Sultan of Atjeh, who had been their unmitigated foe, and put in his place, 102 petty aristocratic rulers each with his own domain. The result was that the new rulers quarrelled with each other and destroyed the unity of the Atjeh people, so that nine years later the Dutch were the victors.

The war in Atjeh did not prevent the Dutch from exploiting the riches of other parts of Sumatra. In the nineteenth century they grew wealthy from dealing in Sumatran timber, tobacco, palm oil and spices. While in the twentieth century, it was neither "golde nor diamants", that produced vast fortunes, but rubber and oil, not only for the Dutch but for the English, the French, the Belgians and the Americans.

When it was found that rubber could be cultivated in Sumatra, many countries advanced capital for such projects, but the most prominent investor was the United States Rubber Company. Joining with a Dutch corporation, a new venture was started. This company acquired 80,000 acres of land for rubber production, thus bringing the largest rubber estates in the world under a single ownership.

And then, as if nature were not satisfied with this gift, but wished to dazzle her admirers even more, oil was discovered. Bitter international rivalry began. The major contest was between the Royal Dutch Oil Company and the Standard Oil Company of New Jersey, then under the direct control of John D. Rockefeller.

The Dutch Company did not want an American competitor in Sumatra, and when Rockefeller tried to obtain an interest in a French company that was already established there, the Government of the Netherlands Indies stepped in and declared that it was ready to deny a concession to any concern controlled by Standard Oil. Whereupon, John D. Rockefeller, who had once declared that he believed the power to make money was a gift of God, launched an attack against his Dutch competitor.

Using a tactic which he had successfully employed in destroying rival oil concerns within the United States, Rockefeller proceeded to cut prices in those markets where Royal Dutch was in competition with Standard Oil. This economic warfare proved so devastating to the interests of the Royal Dutch Oil Company, whose financial position began to deteriorate, that it was glad to call for mercy. The Government of the Netherlands Indies was forced to grant oil concessions to Standard Oil, not only in Sumatra but in Java as well.

After Indonesian independence, many of the rubber estates were divided into smaller holdings, in response to the demands of the Sumatran rubber workers, but the production of oil remained in the hands of four companies; two being subsidiaries of American oil companies; one, a Dutch company and the fourth a joint Indonesian Government-private company enterprise. During the West Irian campaign the Dutch holdings were nationalized, and among the trade unions there was a demand for the nationalization of all oil concerns. This was a cause of uneasiness in the business community, and added to the fuel that the rebels used to build their fire. But whatever the oil companies might have thought, they maintained a position of strict neutrality and refused to pay the tax asked for by the rebels. The policy of the oil companies, like that of Hatta, was to wait and see.

We didn't realize that the Sumatran situation was of such world-wide importance until we arrived in Singapore to find the city swarming with reporters. Every room in every hotel was taken and we would not have found accommodation except for the fact that our reservations had been made in advance. Raffles Hotel was like a huge press room. Reporters were typing, telephoning and cabling. They were interviewing anyone who had come from Sumatra.

The Singapore newspapers, never noted for their restraint, were proclaiming rebel victories daily. As soon as one report proved to be untrue another more sensational story would appear. After the initial shock, we knew there was no reason to be worried as the dispatches in the papers had no relation to what was actually taking place. One reporter, learning that we were from Surabaja, began discussing the rebellion with us, but when we suggested that the Government might win, he was no longer interested in our opinion. Yet that very day Government troops re-captured Pakan Baru, a victory of tremendous importance, because this secured protection of the oil fields belonging to the Caltex Company. The rebels had surrendered with all their equipment, including many cases of arms and ammunition marked *Taiwan*, which had been dropped by a foreign plane only a few hours before the arrival of the Government paratroops.

When this Government victory became known many of the women and children who had been evacuated decided to return. We also flew back to Surabaja, and when we arrived there we learned that the revolt which had begun in Sumatra had spread to Sulawesi, which is not far from East Java, as flying time between the capital of Sulawesi, Makassar and Surabaja is only two hours.

The Government made no secret of its concern over this new development. It was rumoured that Surabaja might be bombed. Because of this there were black-outs and alerts. Once in a while we thought we heard anti-aircraft fire. Military control was strict and since most of the planes had been requisitioned for the air force, the mails were delayed.

Military experts believed that the uprising in Sulawesi would be more difficult to put down than the one in Sumatra. The anti-Government forces were centred in the north-eastern part of the island, whose capital is Menado. The Menadonese, mainly Christian, were favoured by the Dutch. Many of them served as soldiers in the Dutch Army and had fought against the revolution.

Because of the proximity of north-east Sulawesi to the Philippines, it was easy for the rebels to obtain military planes which could be used to bomb ships that plied between the islands. The main problem facing

Government forces was to recapture the airfields. But before this could be accomplished, a number of ships were sunk; insurance rates soared and shipping between the islands was disrupted. The climax came when a Liberty Bomber, piloted by an American mercenary, Allen Lawrence Pope, was shot down while attempting to bomb an unarmed Indonesian vessel.

Government troops were having a rugged time in Sulawesi when they gained an unexpected ally, the people of Makassar and the army stationed there. Makassar, often called the Singapore of East Indonesia, occupies a strategic position on the south-western tip of Sulawesi. The Makassarese are Muslim and have a long history of resistance to the Dutch, beginning in the early eighteenth century when Sultan Hasan Udin fought to preserve his principality. Because Makassar was at that time a free port, "all strange and Moorish nations" came there to trade and the Sultan was provided with "European weapons of fine guns and muskets". But despite these he was defeated, his palace destroyed and in its place the Dutch erected a fortress which they named Rotterdam.

During the 1945 revolution, a pro-Republican uprising took place in Makassar and to quell it a punitive expedition under the leadership of Captain Raymond Westerling was dispatched by the Dutch. About 30,000 Makassarese were put to death, many of them being bundled together and shot in groups of fifty.

Now once again the Makassarese remained loyal to the Indonesian Government. When it became known that the army in Makassar was fighting with Government troops, the rebel leaders in northern Sulawesi surrendered with their entire outfits. In a short time the Government gained complete control over the island.

In Sumatra, the situation also changed, for within the rebel's own stronghold there was serious discontent. In Sasak, north of Bukit Tinggi, veterans of the revolution who had settled there as farmers took up arms against the rebels. Then a battalion under Major Noormathias broke away from the rebel command finding support among the various police units. This was followed by an uprising in Bukit Tinggi itself, where two former members of the Indonesian National Army, Djuhir Mohammed and Ganto Suaro, led forces against the rebels.

Realizing that the military potential of the rebels was crumbling, Government forces planned "Operation August 17th". This involved the army, navy and air force and resulted in the recapture of Padang and Bukit Tinggi. The back of the rebellion was broken.

Chapter Ten

THE REBELLION HAD LOST its initial momentum and the offensive was now with the National Army. Though fighting continued in Sumatra, a period of relative tranquility ensued. It was during this lull that we went, with a number of friends, to witness the Kasada Ceremony.

The head-man of Tosari village told us that the festival, which always takes place in the month of May, would be held at the time of the next full moon, at Bromo, the brooding volcano that lies like a sleeping giant in the heart of East Java. The festivities were to begin at sunset, and on the stroke of midnight there would be a ceremony which belonged, not to the twentieth century, but to that ancient period when animistic beliefs held sway; when man, frightened by the vagaries of the unknown, attempted to appease the elements with sacrifices, so that he might be spared.

Anxious to witness this spectacle, we started on our way the next Sunday morning, driving towards the village of Sukapura, where we planned to spend the evening. It was a glorious May day; the sun shining in a cloudless sky, the air soft and vibrant. For a while we followed the sea-coast where fishing proas and graceful sailing vessels were outlined against tall coconut palms. Then just before reaching a small town with the musical name of Probolinggo, we turned towards the hills.

Unlike the mountainous terrain of other countries, the hills of Java rise unexpectedly from the smooth flowing valleys. It is as though these volcanic mountains had been planted by the farmers, just as they have planted their rice terraces, and with the same artistic ability. It took us less than an hour to cover the twenty-five or so kilometres as the road was paved and in good condition. We must have risen two or three thousand feet by following the tree-lined highway which passed through rice fields and then coffee plantations and then acacia forests.

We reached our first halting place at noon, a pension called Losman Sukapura. It is run by an elderly Chinese lady who lives in the past, when the Dutch gentry patronized her hotel. The living-room of the pension was crowded with knick-knacks, reminiscent of a day that would never return. There was a Dutch clock with the minute hand missing, some chipped blue plates with faded windmills, a pewter mug with an engraving of a Dutch burgher, his ruffled collar hiding his face and an old tile stove that had never been used.

Padding on bare feet, the lady, dressed in black trousers and a black jacket, showed us our room. There was no furniture in it, but six mats had been placed on the floor.

"This is where you are to sleep," she said in Indonesian, speaking with a heavy Dutch accent.

"You mean six people will sleep in this room?" I asked her.

She nodded her head. I was one woman among five men, and unlike Draupadi, the heroine of the *Mahabharata*, who had five husbands, all of whom loved her very much, I had only one, and the thought of sharing a room with so many others caused me some anxiety.

"Njonja," I pleaded, "I think it is unseemly for me to occupy a room with five men."

She winked at me before replying, her wrinkled face becoming quite mischievous, and then said: "It may not be seemly, but it should be interesting," whereupon the Indonesians in our group laughed, but the Indians pretended to be shocked, for it is in keeping with their tradition never to discuss anything concerned with sex in a light-hearted manner.

Before I could answer, the mistress of the Losmen, shrugging her narrow shoulders, said: "Never mind, I will put you with some high-school girls where you will be quite safe."

She showed me to another room where about a dozen young girls were milling about, talking and giggling. As is usual for young people in Java, they wore blouses and skirts rather than Indonesian dress, but all of them had thick, long hair in which they had entwined flowers.

The girls began asking me all kinds of questions, but before I had time to answer, my husband knocked at the door, and then entered. The girls giggled even more when they saw him, but did not speak as they were shy in the presence of a man. My husband suggested that rather than stay in the Losman for the afternoon, we should explore the village from which the Kasada festival was to be approached, the village of Ngadisari. Bidding the girls farewell, I joined the rest of our party and we started out.

This time the highway was unpaved and in many places ungraded. The curves were very sharp and the car could not make the precipitous grade with all of us in it. We had to walk while the driver went ahead.

It took us almost two hours to make the fourteen kilometres, and when we finally reached Ngadisari, we were afraid to return to Sukapura for dinner, so we sent the driver back alone for our sweaters and some food. While waiting we strolled through the village bazaar.

Everyone was dressed for the occasion, especially the children. The little girls had their faces whitened with rice powder to keep away the evil spirits. They were quite timorous and held their scarves over the lower half of their faces, so all we could see were immense brown eyes peering at us with keen interest.

There was one "warung" in the bazaar, which consisted of a wooden counter and a bench placed in front of it. On the counter there were jars of sweets and savouries and duck eggs. Behind the counter there was a rudimentary kitchen with one charcoal stove for cooking food, and another for heating water.

A warung may be characterized as a poor man's outdoor restaurant. But it is more than that, for in the villages of Java, Sumatra and Bali, the warung is an open forum to which anyone can come. Even issues of world importance are discussed. Traditionally the owner is a woman, and she bears the same relationship to her customers as a taxi driver to the citizens of New York.

The owner of this warung was a young and pretty girl, who wore a white Turkish towel wound round her head. When we sat down and ordered coffee, she was not shy, but chatted with us about the festival. The coffee she served was "Kopi Tobruk", black and heavy. She made it by boiling water and coffee grounds together. She told us to let it stand a few moments until the grounds sank to the bottom. But when we tried to drink it, we found that there were so many grounds clustered around the rim of the cup, it was like eating rather than drinking coffee.

Just as we were finishing, it began to rain. Everyone scattered and in a matter of minutes, the bazaar, which had been filled with people was empty. Only the warung girl continued with her work, undisturbed and undeterred by the downpour, her white towel bobbing here and there, like the sail on a fishing boat.

Fortunately, for us, the driver had returned, and so we crept into the car for shelter. We waited almost four hours for the rain to stop and as midnight approached, it began to clear and we could see a wan moon floating in a sky of clouds. Until then, the combination of rain and fog had obscured the view so we felt as though we were isolated in the midst of a great moor.

While we were still waiting, and eating the few sandwiches we had brought with us, a horseman approached. He was riding a sturdy, small pony. Coming near the car, he slid down gracefully from his mount, and then knocked on the car window, which had been closed because of the rain. My husband lowered the window and the horseman said that he had a number of sturdy and sure-footed ponies which we could hire. After some sharp but good-natured bargaining we agreed on a price. The horses were very small but proved capable of carrying us up the steep trail.

The main road from the village to the volcano was thrown open to traffic at exactly midnight. Although those on horseback or afoot were able to get through earlier, the jeeps could not pass until the barricade was removed. There must have been fifty horses and more than a dozen jeeps pressed into service for the occasion, but most of the people were walking. All along the trail we saw people trudging towards the volcano, and a thinner stream returning. Apparently, the entire population of that hill district, known as the Tengger Mountains, and whose people are called the Tenggerese, turned out for the festival.

The women seemed to outnumber the men, and there were many, many children. They were dressed in their best, but it was evident that this was a poor district as there was not much finery. We felt the chill of the midnight air even more as we watched the people huddling up in their thin cotton garments.

For nearly an hour and a half, we climbed upwards, the horses plodding slowly but steadily and the horsemen shouting "djalam" to clear a way for us through the crowds. Finally, we reached a ridge and there below us, like a mirage, lay a sea of black volcanic sand. Looking across this level stretch we could see in the distance one very high peak, Mount Bathok, to the left of which the volcano Bromo was wreathed in smoke.

At the foot of this highest peak there was a cluster of bright lights which we could easily see, although they were more than a kilometre away. The horseman explained that we had to cross the sandy area by a circuitous route, as it was cut by a dry river that made it impossible for the horses to follow the same trail as those going by foot. As we rode across this barren plateau, I asked Hassan, our Indonesian friend: "How did this sea of sand get here?"

Smiling, he replied: "Once upon a time a god lived on the highest mountain of Java, Mount Smeru, with his only daughter, Princess Juwitha. Near Smeru is the Bromo, and on this volcano lived an ugly

106

giant with a noble heart. This giant set eyes upon Juwitha and wanted to marry her. Juwitha, who had never seen another man, fell in love with him.

"The giant of Bromo went to the god of Mount Smeru and asked for the hand of his daughter. But the king did not want his daughter to marry anyone so ugly. However he was afraid to speak the truth and so he replied, 'If within a single night, you can dig a ditch around Bromo, wide enough and deep enough to protect Mount Smeru, then I will allow my daughter to become your wife.'

"That very evening the giant began to dig the ditch, using a big coconut shell. The giant worked hard, hour after hour, strong in the knowledge of his love, and it looked as though he would be able to fulfil the command. But the God of Mount Smeru thought of a trick. He went to the place, where at dawn the women stamp the paddy with heavy wooden poles. Taking one of the poles, the god began pounding the wood block, so the cocks, who heard the stamping, thought it was morning and began to crow.

"The giant heard the crowing of the cocks. He was frightened. He looked up at the sky which was not yet red, but in his fright the coconut shell fell from his hand, and it became a mountain, Mount Bathok, which stands at the edge of the sea of sand. Then the giant himself fell and became a stone. The god of Mount Smeru was satisfied, but soon his lovely daughter Juwitha died of a broken heart, and the god shut himself up in his room and was never seen again. Often the people are reminded of him, because when he becomes angry over the loss of his daughter, the mountain roars and throws off flames and lava, bringing death and destruction to the human beings who live on its slopes. And that is the legend of the sea of sand," Hassan concluded.

After riding for another twenty minutes, we came to the lights. There were crowds of people everywhere, encircled by pillars of smoke. Here the sea of sand was like a carnival. Our attention was attracted by a group of men and women standing around two flag poles and an acetylene lamp. On one pole the red and white flag of Indonesia was flying, while on the other, a rainbow-hued Buddhist flag had been draped. In the centre of the circle there was an image of the Buddha, and next to it, a Buddhist priest, dressed in the traditional saffron-coloured robe, barefoot with his head shaven, was lecturing to the audience. Beside him on the ground was his begging bowl, signifying the fact that he had given up all worldly possessions, and was forced to beg for his food.

We listened to the monk for a while and then walked over to the place where many men and women were standing, holding in their arms baskets of flowers, ears of corn and live chickens. Seated in front of this crowd was a line of praying figures, accompanied by assistants. These young men were pouring incense on the small fires flickering in front of them. The smell of the incense brought back memories of Hindu temples in India.

The priests were blessing the offerings that the people had brought. As they blessed each item they chanted, and listening carefully I realized that the prayers were in Sanscrit. Turning to one of the priests, or "dukuns" as they are called, I asked him to whom he was praying. He answered:

"We pray to Brahma, for that is the true name of the volcano that is now known as Bromo. Who was Brahma but the god of creation, for we know that when the divine life substance was about to put forth the universe, the cosmic waters grew a thousand-petalled lotus of pure gold, radiant as the sun, and this lotus opened to give birth to the creator of the world, Brahma."

Seeing that our friend Jasbir Singh was watching us, I asked him: "How did Brahma come to Java?" Without a flicker of a smile he answered nonchalantly: "He came from India on his gander, of course. How else does Brahma the creator travel?"

I laughed, for in Hindu mythology, just as Indra rides on an elephant, Shiva on a garuda, Shiva's son on a peacock, and Devi on a lion, so does Brahma soar through the air on a wonderful gander, which can, like Sputnik, take him around the world in a matter of hours. So it was quite understandable that if Brahma wished to tour Java, he would arrive on the back of his gander.

"Now, seriously, Jasbir, how did Hinduism find its way to the Tengger Mountains?"

"During the second century," he replied, "many traders from South India migrated to Indonesia, settling in Java, Sumatra and Kalimantan. Some were Buddhists and others Hindus. Accompanying these merchants were Brahman priests, who influenced the kings of Indonesia to become Hindus. And Hinduism remained the religion of the court until the end of the fourteenth century when armed conflict broke out between Islam and the Hindu Madjapahit Empire. Many Hindus refused to be converted. The nobles and priests fled to Bali, but the ordinary people withdrew to the Tengger highlands, where they have continued the practice of Hinduism. Although the Tenggerese do not believe in reincarnation, their caste system and calendar are similar to those of the Balinese."

While he was speaking we heard shouting, which now became so loud that Jasbir's last words were drowned out. We noticed a group of men who were talking excitedly. We thought another prayer meeting must be in progress, but when we came nearer we saw that this was far from a religious ceremony, for the only prayers were addressed to dice that were being thrown by one man and then another. Instead of numbers, the dice bore curious symbols, and the same symbols appeared on squares painted on a piece of cloth spread on the ground.

It was a weird scene, the sea of sand alive with people praying, playing dice, and eating. The oil-fed torches cast strange shadows. One expected the witches of Macbeth to appear before the cauldrons of steaming food. The whole atmosphere had a quality of unreality, as though it were a stage set which would be struck before the dawn.

It was two in the morning when we began our final trek to the volcano. We climbed for half an hour towards the Bromo and we could make out a stream of lights stretching from the sea of sand right to the top. Hundreds of people were climbing in an unending line to the peak, and an equal number were coming down, so there was constant confusion, as clusters of those moving upwards collided with groups that were descending along the steep, narrow trail. The men going up carried sacrificial offerings that had been blessed by the dukuns.

"There are countless stories about the Kasada ceremony," Hassan remarked. "Originally, it was supposed to have commemorated the death of Buddha, but many Tenggerese believe it is an honour to Kusumo, who flung himself into the crater, and whose soul still dwells in the Tengger Mountains.

"The legend is that one of the last kings of the Madjapahit empire, fearing that he would have to accept Islam, fled with his daughter to the Tenggerese highlands. Realizing that his days were numbered, the king arranged a marriage between his daughter and a Brahman priest.

"It was a happy marriage, but when, after three years, they had no children, the priest went to the crater of Bromo and beseeched the gods to heed his prayer and grant him sons and daughters. The gods, having listened to his plea, told him he would have twenty-five children, but when the youngest son reached the age of fifteen he was to be sacrificed.

"Twenty-five sons and daughters were born. But the happiness of the priest and his princess-wife was spoiled, for their youngest boy,

Kusumo, was the handsomest and the finest, and he was the one whom they would have to sacrifice.

"When that dreadful day arrived, the parents hesitated, but Kusumo, who knew of his fate, was filled with courage. He took leave of his father and mother, and climbing Mount Bromo, flung himself into the crater exactly at midnight. The boy's last message to his family was to ask them to visit the crater once a year, and bring him food and flowers. Since then, the Tenggerese, on the twelfth month of the Hindu-Javanese calendar, for 'kesada' means twelve, go to the volcano at midnight to offer food and flowers."

Even now as we climbed the Bromo we could pretend, or was it really pretence, that the gentle spirit of Kusumo hovered over us. And as we did not wish him to go away, we were careful not to utter the words "hot or cold, hungry or thirsty", because on this pilgrimage, if such words are uttered, then "ash-rains, heat waves, thunderstorms and floods" will ensue, and Kusumo will be forced to flee.

The trail was growing more and more precipitous and we found the climb difficult. At first we rejected the idea of being assisted by our guides, but finally we let them pull us up with the help of a metal ring. Each individual held to one side of the ring, whilst the guide grasped the other side. We were hoisted up like marionettes on a string. Even with this assistance, the ascent was so steep, I did not think I would be able to make it.

Half-way up the slope we saw what seemed to be a thick hedge of trees at the top. The trees swayed back and forth as though moved by an invisible wind. But when we reached the top, we were horrified to find that what had looked like a hedge from the distance, was in reality, thousands of people perched on the razor-thin edge of the crater.

The brim of the crater was so narrow that everyone was swaying slightly to keep his balance; and while we were watching this frightening scene, one poor chap slipped and tumbled into the crater. The crater inside was even steeper than the one we had just managed to negotiate, and we feared that the man who had fallen was doomed. Fortunately for him, he was rescued by a group of dark shapes who were clambering around inside retrieving some of the food and money that had been thrown down. These men, who were collecting the offerings for their personal use, were not considered to be blaspheming the gods; for the Tenggerese believe that the gods are only interested in having the essence; material things are for the living.

Almost a mile down inside the crater was the raging volcano. Billowing clouds of smoke sometimes hid the fire, but when they were blown aside, the bright red flames emerged. We were gazing into the Forge of Vulcan. Whenever the wind blew towards us, our throats burned from the sulphurous fumes. Here, we were seeing a force which was beyond the control of man. This dragon which breathed fire and flame had not been tamed, not even in our atomic age. No wonder, that in the olden times, people felt it was necessary to placate the evil spirits of the volcano.

To appease these spirits was especially important in Indonesia, for the Archipelago is the most volcanic region in the world. There are more than four hundred volcanoes, a hundred of which are active. Sometimes centuries pass and the volcanoes remain passive. During that time the Indonesians consider them as friends. Because of the deposits of black volcanic ash, the soil is enriched. Countless rivers carrying the alluvium down the mountain slopes to the plains below, make the land so fertile that the farmers are able to harvest two and sometimes three crops of paddy a year.

Then without warning, they erupt and wreak havoc. In 1883, when the famous Indonesian volcano, Krakatau, erupted, the explosion was so tremendous that some of the ashes circulated two or even three times around the world before settling. In England, Lord Tennyson took up his pen to commemorate this event in poetry. A Spanish friend of ours said that his father told him special masses were held in Madrid because the sky was obscured by clouds of dust and the people were frightened.

A quarter of a century later, Bali's most active volcano, the Gunung Batur, erupted causing severe damage. "At that time, the lava engulfed the village of Batur, which lies on the beautiful lake with the same name, but stopped at the very gates of the temple. The villagers took this miracle as a good omen and continued to live there." But in 1926, the temple was buried under a river of lava in another eruption. Despite this, many Balinese still live in the shadow of the Gunung Batur, defying its power with the indestructible optimism of man.

And now the night was over and dawn was breaking. We had to begin the long journey back to the village of Ngadisari where our car and driver were waiting. From the village we planned to return to the Losman Sukapura for a few hours' rest before driving to Surabaja. The early morning sun, casting its brilliant rays over the volcano, dispelled the magic that we had felt the night before. Bromo was stripped of its all-embracing power by the searching eye of the day; even as in our time superstitions have wilted under the searching light of science.

The people who were slowly climbing down the precipitous incline looked pale and wan, and a few of the children were whimpering. Small pieces of rotting fruit and torn petals of faded flowers marked our way; all that remained of the beautiful sacrificial offerings that had been carried up the night before with such loving care.

The sea of sand was empty and desolate. Here and there a few fragments of cloth printed with strange symbols, reminded us of the gambling that had taken place during the night hours. The Buddhist and Hindu priests had gone away, taking the flags and the image of Buddha, but the flag pole was still standing, naked and forlorn amidst the black volcanic sand.

The shops in the village bazaar were closed, but the warung was open, and the young girl, with the white Turkish towel wound around her head, was as busy as ever. We had a cup of coffee which revived our spirits, and then we climbed into the car. When we reached the Losman Sukapura, exhaustion claimed us, and we slept without removing our clothes. A few hours later, my husband woke me, saying: "We'd better start for home." Still half asleep, I tried to think where home could be, and then I remembered, we were not going home to Bombay, India, and we were not going home to Rangoon, Burma, but this time it was home to Surabaja, Indonesia.

Administration building of Airlangga University

Girl students parading during the West Irian crisis

The Hindu Museum in the village of Trawulen, which was the capital of the Madjapahit empire. The museum is an exact reproduction of a fourteenth-century building

Tenggerese at the Kasada ceremony with offerings for the Hindu gods of Mount Bromo

Chapter Eleven

FOR THE NEXT FEW MONTHS we enjoyed the luxury of being cool, for June, July and August is the pleasantest time of the year. It is the Javanese winter. The days seemed warm to us, but mothers bundled their children in heavy clothes, and in the evening the ladies wore long-sleeved dresses or woollen stoles over their kebajas.

Early in September the heat began again. Fortunately, we were invited to a conference that was being held in Bandung, which is never as hot as Surabaja. The Conference, called by the Ministry of Education, was for the purpose of acquainting foreign experts with some of the problems that Indonesia faces in this field. We decided that on the way to Bandung, we would stop at Jogjakarta and also visit the famous Buddhist stupa, the Borobudur.

As we drove along the same road which had brought us to Surabaja, we were in less of a hurry, and so we noticed a huge stone giant standing close to the highway, so close that he gave the appearance of being a malevolent traffic officer just waiting to pounce on an erring driver. Around his left shoulder there was a sculptured cobra and on his head he wore an elaborate crown. Long, decorative ear-rings fell from his cauliflower ears to his shoulders.

Fascinated by this strange apparition, we stopped to take a closer look. He seemed a likeable chap but hardly a beauty as two fangs protruded from his mouth. Opposite him was his equally unattractive twin, and the two faced each other in frozen hatred.

Just behind the demons there was a curious wooden building with an enormous roof shaped like a haystack. On top of the roof there was a six-pointed star and above this a small umbrella, symbolizing the Buddhist priesthood. The roof of this strange building was made of millions of small tiles held in place by many wires.

We entered the main room and saw among the curios a striking sculptured head of a young girl carrying a pot of water. She had a long, thin nose, high cheek bones and deep-set eyes, characteristics of an Indian beauty. After gazing at her in delight, we walked around looking at the old, faded maps; some burnished armour that might have come from England or from Hollywood and a few unimpressive Chinese porcelain vases.

Then we meandered outside and there on the ground, strewn about carelessly, were several fine stone images of Hindu gods. Shiva, Ganesh, Lakshmi and Krishna were lying side by side in varying stages of decay. Farther back we noticed another building, and when we entered we were astounded for everywhere we looked there were baskets and baskets of rubble. The baskets were made of wire and had been placed on shelves that reached from the floor to the ceiling. The rubble in them was all one colour, a reddish brown, like the soil of Georgia.

We were so engrossed by this strange sight that we did not hear a man enter the building. He startled us with his greeting, and then he said: "I am sure you will find it difficult to believe that the pieces of clay contained in these baskets were once part of the great Hindu Madjapahit Empire, for it was here in this very village of Trawulan, that the Prime Minister of Madjapahit, Gadjah Mada, directed the activities of the kingdom."

"Then this is the Hindu Museum that we noticed on our road map."

"Yes, but it is not in very good condition," he replied, "but we are hoping that some day we will be able to reconstruct a fourteenth-century city from the rubble that has been gathered from around here. The large bamboo house you saw as you entered is an exact replica of the type of dwelling that existed at the time of Madjapahit."

"And all of this," I said, pointing to the rubble in the baskets, "represents what was once the capital of an empire."

"Exactly," he replied with a note of pride in his voice as though he were able to visualize the whole scene as it had existed some six hundred years ago.

We thanked him for his kindness, and as we were leaving, I took one last look. Could all those bits and pieces be put together again. Surely it would take many skilful archaeologists years of patient work before such a task could be completed. And, if they succeeded would the real spirit of Madjapahit be revived. This was a dramatic period in Indonesian history when all of the main islands were united under the great Gadjah Mada, in whose hands the heavy task of protecting the world came to rest.

Gadjah Mada was an officer in the royal bodyguard of King Hayam Wuruk, a weak man, described by his court poet, Prapança, as being "without cares or worries. He indulges in all pleasures. All beautiful maidens in Jangalla and Kediri are selected for him . . . and those who are captured in foreign countries, the prettiest girls are brought to his harem."

The King's dalliance resulted in his soldiers revolting. He fled from the palace and it was Gadjah Mada who helped find him a hiding place and then crushed the rebellion. For this he was promoted to "Patih", prime minister, in 1331. Shrewd, resourceful and not given to the same interests as the King, he ruled with an iron hand. During his lifetime, trade and diplomatic relations with foreign countries flourished. And it was during his tenure of office that the official motto of modern Indonesia, "Bhinneka Tunggal Ika," Unity in Diversity, was first used.

After the death of Gadjah Mada in 1364, the structure he created gradually disintegrated. The King did not have an "official son", for his queen had given birth to a daughter. Rather than allow a woman to rule Hayam Wuruk divided his empire among the many sons of his unofficial wives. With this gesture he destroyed the unity of the empire. His sons fought against each other for the throne so that East and Central Java were turned into a battle-field. And into this arena of conflict came a new and virile force, Islam.

Mohammedanism, for some time, had been finding converts among the traders living in the large sea ports. They were irked by the caste system. Belonging to the Vaisya caste, which was considerably lower than that of the priests and the nobility, the merchants chafed under the many restrictions placed upon them by Hinduism. Because of caste they were unable to marry into the upper class. Even their wealth failed to unlock this door. But Islam emphasized the importance of the individual. It rejected caste. It gave the necessary ideological basis for the welding of money and aristocracy.

Furthermore, the Islamic teachers challenged the absolute power of the petty nobles. They were the principal, if not the only, opponents of secular government, who refused to become the tools of princely authority. At the same time they were able to convert some of the Hindu princes, who then challenged the rulers of Madjapahit. Backed by the wealth of the traders, these Muslim princes won and the last flowering of Hinduism on Java was destroyed. The very meaning of "Madjapahit" seems appropriate, for here indeed was a harvest of "bitter fruit".

When we arrived in Jogjakarta, as it is officially called, or Jogja, as it is affectionately known to the people of Java, we realized that the traditions of Madjapahit had not vanished. For like this medieval empire, Jogjakarta is also a kingdom based on an agrarian economy. The court has always been the nucleus around which the life of the city revolved. The people have for centuries lived in small wooden houses, behind the protective walls of the city, and they have planted paddy and devoted their spare time to handicrafts. When the Soviet Prime Minister, Nikita Khrushchev, visited Jogjakarta in 1960, he sensed its feudal nature, and when shown some of Jogja's most beautiful hand-made batiks, remarked that they were too expensive, not in terms of price but in the amount of labour that had gone into their production.

Jogjakarta has a medieval air, for with the exception of the new Gadjah Mada University and the complex of modern houses built at the time of the Colombo Conference, there are no modern structures. Like the physical aspect of the city, the social life reflects ancient customs. It is not unusual to see people bowing; children to adults, adults to their elders, and elders to officials. This formalism is also preserved in the Javanese language which is spoken most fluently and in its purest form by the people of Jogja.

A friend of ours, one of the many princesses of Jogjakarta, whose grandfather, the Sultan, had thirty wives and eighty children, once said to me:

"I wish you could speak Javanese. I don't like Bahasa Indonesia. It is vulgar and the sounds are harsh. Javanese is like music, being derived from Sanscrit, which is often chanted rather than spoken. For me, Javanese is more than a language, it is a way of life, mirroring our social customs. When a servant speaks to me she uses high Javanese while I answer her in low Javanese. But if I speak to my father it is in high Javanese and he will answer in low Javanese. It is only among equals, both in age and rank, that one may use the middle form of the language. Thus, through the spoken word, the social standing of an individual is made known."

Listening to her, I remembered that Siti had told me how much she disliked Javanese, precisely because it was undemocratic and sharpened the stratification between classes. These two women, the princess and Siti, represented groups in the community who had always been in conflict; those who revered the ancient culture and wanted social and economic distinctions to remain as they were, and those who were imbued with the revolutionary spirit and wanted changes made in the social order. The princess, with her charm and grace, her polished courtly manners and love for Javanese was a typical product of the royalty. While Siti, equally charming, but rough-hewn and earthy, typified the villagers and peasants who had been exploited for centuries by the nobility.

But in Jogjakarta, unlike the other principalities ruled by the rajas, there were times when the court and the village were brought together in a common cause; when the interests of the nobles and the people coincided. Unlike the Sunans of Solo, the rulers of Jogja often resisted foreign encroachment. Thus, Lieut.-Governor Raffles, who was welcomed in Solo, had a very different reception in Jogjakarta when he arrived there in December of 1811.

The Sultan of Jogja had deliberately arranged the chairs so that Sir Stamford would be seated at a lower level than himself. Realizing immediately the subtle implication of this arrangement, Raffles insisted that the chairs be changed. The courtiers became angry and drew their swords, and in Java, if a man unsheathes his kris, it is considered cowardly for him not to use it. A clash was avoided, but Sir Stamford admitted that the treaty he wrested from the Sultan was really an armed negotiation, and that his own behaviour was not noble but prudent.

In June of 1812, the Sultan revolted. Raffles and Major-General Gillespie who were in Semarang heard the news and then left immediately for Jogjakarta, "with a small escort composed of part of the 14th Regiment of Bengal Light Infantry, the 3rd Volunteer Battalion, some gunners and two troops of dragoons. The main military force, under Lieut.-Colonel McLeod, was to follow with most of the artillery". They reached Jogja on June 17th.

The next day, June 18th, heavy fighting commenced. The people destroyed the bridges, tore up the roads and fought with hand-made weapons. But two days later the Sultan was defeated and his kraton was given over to the army to loot. "It provided a rich booty in which every officer and man shared in his degree."

When the Dutch returned to power in 1816, they tried to insure their command over Jogjakarta by placing a weak and corrupt man on the throne. In doing so, they set the stage for the appearance of one of the great heroes of Indonesia, Prince Diponegoro. He was the elder brother and rightful heir, but because of his strong character and unbending hostility to Dutch rule, his rightful inheritance was usurped.

Rather than remain idle at court, Prince Diponegoro visited different villages in Central Java. Soon the people began to think of him as a saint. It was said that a magic kris had been sent to him from Allah and that this weapon would protect him from death. He was given the title of Prince Liberator who had been chosen by God to drive the invaders from his country.

When he raised the red and white banner of revolt, in 1825, the response was tremendous. The military might of the Prince became so great that Holland had to send a special division to Java composed of 3,000 infantry, troopers and artillerymen, to crush the rebellion. For five years the fighting continued. The villagers and soldiers remained faithful, but the effects of such prolonged warfare combined with an epidemic of cholera which ravaged Central Java, weakened their ability to continue the struggle. Slowly the Dutch armies gained the initiative.

The Prince was a master of guerrilla tactics and avoided any battles in the open field. But near Magelang, within the shadow of the Boro-budur, he was forced into direct conflict with the Dutch, and he and his army suffered a great defeat. After Magelang a few of Prince Dipo-negoro's ranking officers defected. In 1830, the Prince was tricked into submission by General de Kock, Commander of the Dutch forces, who, under the pretext of discussing peace terms, arrested the Prince.

Prince Diponegoro is considered an exemplary hero of his country, and the red and white banner which he carried has become the national flag of Indonesia. Nor have the legends about the Prince Liberator diminished, for not long ago an item appeared in the daily newspaper, which read as follows:

"A selamatan was held at Ungaran, Central Java, in order to appease the malicious spirits that have been causing trouble at the ancient Detention House of Indonesia's National Hero, Prince Diponegoro. The police inspector explained that the Detention House could no longer be used as a residence for the police because the building was haunted by the evil spirits of those who had unjustly imprisoned the Prince."

And today, again, a Sultan of Jogjakarta, Hamengku Buwono IX, is a national hero. When he was a young man he was known as Prince Gusti Daradjatun. He was sent to Holland for his studies and upon his return to Indonesia he was met in Djakarta by his many brothers and his father, the reigning Sultan. His father was seriously ill and on the train offered his kris to his son, a gesture symbolizing the transfer of power.

At first he refused. Although he was the son of the queen, and therefore legally entitled to the throne, he told his father that he would be willing to defer in favour of one of his older brothers. The Prince then asked each of his brothers whether he would like to become the sultan. Each brother refused, assuring Prince Gusti Daradjatun that he was the one who should become the Sultan of Jogjakarta in the event of the death of their father. It was only when he had received this pledge of loyalty from his brothers, that he accepted the kris from his father, who died before the train reached Jogjakarta.

In Jogja, all arrangements had been made for the funeral of the old Sultan and for the installation of the new one. Prince Gusti Daradjatun became Sultan Hamengku Buwono IX, and as soon as he was declared the Sultan, the Dutch asked him to sign a document curtailing some of his power. He refused to sign, and told the officials that not only would he resist restriction of his prerogatives, but that he would not even agree to the narrow powers that his father had been forced to accept. Instead, he wanted all those rights that had been enjoyed by his grandfather.

When the Dutch officials heard his terms they became angry, and shortly thereafter began to sound out his brothers with the hope that one of them could be persuaded to challenge Hamengku Buwono's right to the throne. But as each brother had already pledged his fidelity, not one was willing to enter such a conspiracy. The tactic of divide and rule having failed, the Dutch were forced to confer upon the new Sultan all of the powers that his grandfather possessed.

This was the beginning of his feud with the Dutch, which reached its climax when Jogjakarta became the capital of the Republic during the revolutionary struggle from 1946 to 1950. It was from Jogjakarta that the fight for independence was directed, and during those crucial years, the Sultan played a decisive role. Like Diponegoro, he sold many of his possessions to feed, clothe and arm the soldiers. Behind the high walls of his kraton constant political meetings were held.

When the Dutch captured Jogjakarta, the Sultan led the boycott which paralysed activities within the city because all civilian officers refused to obey rules or accept work. Later this boycott spread to all of Central Java. The Dutch let it be known that if the Sultan called off the boycott, he would be rewarded with a vast area which he could administer. The Sultan did not respond to the offer and refused to meet any Dutch negotiators. "Finally, after General Spoor, the Netherlands Commander-in-Chief, threatened to enter the kraton doors in a tank, the Sultan agreed to grant him a ten-minute interview. However, the only subject the Sultan wished to discuss was the departure of the Dutch troops from Jogjakarta."

In recognition of his services to the Republic, the Sultan was later granted the special territory of Jogjakarta. Here he instituted various reforms, including the right of all citizens in his special District, who were over eighteen years of age, to vote for the Local People's Council of Representatives, which now has a majority of members from the Communist Party.

Although the Sultan has engaged in many democratic political activities, he is still a ruling monarch and lives like one, in a walled palace, where he is entertained by gamelan music and dancing girls. Married four times, he still does not have a wife, for he has yet to wed a girl who is from a lineage as royal as his own. Until he does so, he is technically unmarried and none of his children are legally entitled to the throne.

While visiting his kraton, which is one of the finest in Java, we happened to be near the women's quarters, when we noticed a group of beautiful girls approaching. One was carrying a pot of tea; another, a jug of hot water; the third, a bowl of sugar and the fourth, a pitcher of milk. They walked in single file and the loveliest girl of them all carried a golden umbrella, held high as a victorious banner with which she was trying to protect the tea from the sun. When we asked the guard where they were going he said they were bringing the Sultan his morning tea; the same Sultan who had just flown home to pledge his loyalty to the Central Government against the Sumatran rebels.

Chapter Twelve

As WE DROVE towards the Borobudur, it seemed that the green-ness of Central Java was like a symphony. As in the music of Bach, there are endless variations on the same theme. There is the deep green of the trees, the emerald green of the ferns, the blue-green of the sugar cane, the light-green of the corn, and the yellow-green of the paddy fields as they lie in precise geometric figures over the countryside. And it is from this carpet of green that the Borobudur rises, its brownish, weatherbeaten stones standing out harshly against the lush green of the hill upon which it has rested for over a thousand years.

The Borobudur is not a pagoda, for the Buddhists do not come there to pray. It is a "stupa" such as is found throughout Buddhist countries. Ceylon, Burma, Thailand and Cambodia, where historic events in the life of Buddha are commemorated and sacred relics of the Buddha himself are enshrined.

When the Buddha died in the north Indian village of Kusinagara, twenty-five hundred years ago, many of his followers sent messages to the Mallas of Kusinagara, asking for a part of his remains. But the Mallas refused, declaring: "We will not give away any part of the remains of the Exalted One." It was then that a wise man named Drona rebuked the Mallas, saying to them:

"Hear, gracious Sirs, the word I have to say,
Forbearance was the teaching of the Buddha,
Shall the remains of him who was the best of beings
Become the cause of strife and wounds of war.
Let us unite in friendly harmony to mark eight portions.
Let stupas spring widespread in every land.
That in the light of the World mankind may trust."

This advice of Drona was followed, and all the kings and nobles made a stupa in every land, and none was more beautiful than the one created by the Javanese Sailendra kings, known as the Borobudur.

Each stupa had the same basic architectural design, that of a dome, representing a microcosm of the universe, in which the relics of the

Buddha were placed. In its most primitive form the "core of the stupa was of unburnt brick, and the outer face of burnt brick, covered with a thick layer of plaster. The stupa was crowned by an umbrella of wood or stone, and was surrounded by a wooden fence enclosing a path for the ceremonial clockwise circumambulation (pradaksina) which was the chief form of reverence paid to the relics within."

Gradually, the stupa became larger and more ornate, and one of the famous stupas of Ceylon is larger than an Egyptian pyramid. Furthermore, each stupa reflected the national heritage and culture, so the stupas of Burma were not like those built in Ceylon, and the Thai stupas differed from those constructed in China. Most unique of all is the Borobudur.

Seen from a distance, the Borobudur has a clumsy, almost ungainly appearance. Rising stone upon stone, tier upon tier, against a background of mountains, it does not seem to have any architectural unity. Unlike the first sight of the Sanchi stupa of India, which is breathtaking because of its elegant lines and perfect proportions, the Borobudur does not produce an impression of instantaneous, compelling beauty. It is a cameraman's despair. A French photographer, who visited the stupa gave vent to his displeasure by crying out in typical Gallic fashion:

"O disappointing Borobudur: I didn't know what to make of it. A shapeless mass of carved stone, without architectural outline and devoid of grandeur. Three times I walked around the monument, camera in hand, without finding a satisfactory angle."

But despite its unphotogenic exterior, the Borobudur leaves a final impression of magnificence and splendour rarely encountered anywhere in the world. Its very size is awe-inspiring. The base is about 400 feet in width. The substructure rises about fifty feet above the stupa level and the apex of the main stupa's pinnacle reaches almost 138 feet into the air. It is estimated that more than two million cubic feet of stone were used to construct the edifice, and this took place in the ninth century when every operation had to be done by hand.

Drawing nearer to the Borobudur, one is impressed by the fearful damage the elements have wrought throughout the centuries. Although the people who built the stupa had mastered the art of creation, they knew nothing about the science of preservation. Much of the Borobudur was constructed from material that was unable to withstand the heavy wind and rain that accompanies the monsoon season. On every level there is evidence of decay. Many of the walls are sagging, and the steps leading to the summit are cracked and broken. Creeping vines and moss have invaded the terraces. But even though time has been merciless in its destructive activities, enough remains for the visitor to be wonder-struck by the richness of visual delights that unfold before him.

Directly above the base of the Borobudur, there is a series of four hundred and thirty-two Buddhas, each one placed in a niche. The sculptors have captured a universality of feature and expression, so that the images do not seem to belong to any one country but to all mankind.

The next terrace, known as the first gallery, has the largest number and most exquisite examples of bas-relief carvings. There are four galleries adorned with friezes, and every inch of the walls and balustrades are covered with relievos, a total length of more than 5,085 feet of continuous frieze ornamentation.

The only three-dimensional carvings are those of the Buddha and the decorative animals such as the lions guarding the stupa and the gargoyle-like structures which were designed for the practical purpose of controlling the flow of rain-water. Although these are wonderful examples of sculpture, the outstanding work of art at the Borobudur is the series of bas-relief carvings depicting the life of Buddha.

Buddha's life was a simple one, although over the centuries, it has become enshrouded in legend and symbolism. He was the only son of a royal family residing in northern India, close to Nepal. His given name was Siddhartha and his clan name was Gautama. As a boy he was strong, handsome and intelligent. When he grew up he married a beautiful princess and had one son. Surrounded by luxury, he did not know that others were less fortunate, and his father did everything possible to protect him from the sordid realities of life. But on four occasions, the Prince left the palace and came in contact with a different world than the one in which he lived.

On his first encounter, the Prince met an old man, and he realized that he too was not immune to growing old; then he saw a sick man and he knew that he too was liable to the dangers of illness; then he saw a corpse and he understood that he too must die; and finally he encountered an ascetic with a peaceful countenance who had adopted the traditional way of seekers of religious truth. The Prince then resolved to overcome old age, sickness and death by following the example of the holy man from whom he learned that truth makes a human being independent of the temporary trials and fleeting pleasures of the world.

Against the wishes of his father, he renounced his right to the throne, and went into the forest where he spent six years in meditation. When he found his enlightenment, he declared: "I shall go to Banares where I will light the lamp that will bring light into the world. I will go to Banares and beat the drums that will awaken mankind. I shall go to Banares and there I shall teach the law."

What was to be the nature of his teachings? In an age when Hinduism was most orthodox and the social system rigidly fixed, the Buddha decried caste. He said:

> "One does not become a brahmana by birth.
> One does not become an outcast by birth.
> One becomes a brahmana by act.
> One becomes an outcast by act."

The philosophy of the Buddha was based on his solicitude for the common man. He spoke for the vast masses of the peasantry, the backbone of an agricultural economy. For them he was the Compassionate Buddha.

In an age when the women were considered as chattels, the Buddha spoke for them too. His greatest disciples were women, and it was the women who remained his most faithful followers, for long after the kings abandoned Buddhism and returned to the practice of Hinduism, their wives and daughters remained staunch Buddhists.

Among other followers were the merchants and traders, who sailed over the Asian world, carrying the message of Buddha. And one of the panels at Borobudur shows a small ship coming towards Java from India, carrying fifteen passengers and an image of the Buddha.

At the age of eighty, on the banks of the River Hiranyavati, in a grove of Sala trees, the Buddha had a bed prepared, for he knew that he had reached the end of his earthly life. Seeing his disciple Ananda weep, the Buddha said to him: "Do not weep, do not despair, Ananda. From all that he loves man must part. How could it be that what is born, what is subject to instability should not pass? Maybe, you were thinking, 'we have no longer a master'. That must not be, O Ananda. The doctrine I have preached to you is your master."

These were the Buddha's last words before he died, or as the Buddhists say, "His spirit sank into the depths of mystic absorption and when he had attained to that degree where all thought, all conception disappears, when the consciousness of individuality ceases, he entered the supreme Nirvana."

Each panel of the galleries represents a scene from one of the incidents in the life of the Buddha. It is difficult to decide which panel is the most carefully wrought or the most inspiring. Each one has its charm and captivating grace. There is a relievo showing Queen Maya, the mother of Buddha, being carried to the Lumbini gardens where the Prince was born. Another panel depicts Buddha as Prince Siddhartha, standing gracefully with his bow and arrow in hand, taking part in an archery contest, so that by displaying his skill, he might win the beautiful Yasodhara.

There are many different carvings representing the "four encounters". The finest is that of the Prince meeting the holy man. When we studied this panel, we felt as though we could actually hear the Prince saying: "Honoured Sir, I pray you to tell me what manner of man you are," to which the pilgrim answered: "Great Prince, I am called a mendicant, one who has left the world and its ways and has forsaken friends and home, in order to find deliverance." And then the young Prince asked: "What must I do to reach this state?" And the pilgrim replied: "Illustrious youth, if you can learn to regard the desires of the flesh as transitory, if you can think no evil and do none, but rather, do good to all living creatures, then you will be in the way of becoming a homeless one."

Even the farewell of the Prince to his beloved wife and son, has been portrayed. He stands at the doorway of his consort's chamber watching her as she sleeps on a bed strewn with jasmin petals. He is longing to go to her, and in this carving his desire becomes a palpable, living force. But he restrains himself, reasoning: "If I lift my hand and take my son, she will awaken, and perhaps I shall not go. Rather will I return when my mission is accomplished. For never again will I partake of the pleasures of the senses."

There are many friezes portraying the Buddha's struggle to find enlightenment. There is one in which the daughters of the evil Mara try to tempt him. After seeing these voluptuous women, with their large eyes, curvaceous lips, rounded breasts, slender waists and heavy hips, one can understand how much he was tempted, for even in stone they appear irresistible.

In another relievo the Buddha appears sick and emaciated, for he had been fasting. Later, realizing that this type of asceticism would not bring him closer to truth, he abandoned it, explaining to his disciples: "The life of carnal pleasure is ignoble, contrary to the spiritual life, unworthy and vain. But a life of austerities is also sorrowful, unworthy and vain."

After this decision the Buddha broke his fast and accepted a dish of milk and rice from Sujata, the daughter of a cowherd. In this, the most beautiful of all panels, Sujata's gracious act is portrayed, and this lovely, innocent girl becomes immortal.

Climbing upwards, above the decorated galleries, there are three main circular terraces, plain and unadorned, except for seventy-two trellised stupas, each containing an image of the Buddha. These small stupas are of stone lattice-work, and through the apertures, the Buddhas can be seen, half in sunlight and half in shadow. Although the statues seem to be identical, in each one the hands are in a different position, the fingers poised to represent various signs or mudras as they are termed in the classical Indian dance drama.

Whether by design or by accident, one of the small stupas has been broken open, so that the whole figure of the Buddha can be seen. It is as though he were released from a dark and gloomy prison. Now free and unhindered, he is able to look down upon the smooth-flowing landscape of Central Java, where the farmers cultivate their rice just as their ancestors did in the ninth century when the Borobudur was built.

On the highest terrace of all, rises a giant dome. It is austere and without ornamentation because it represents the final phase of the Buddha's life when he reached Nirvana.

Looking down from this great height, it is hard to believe that the Dutch did not know of the existence of the Borobudur, and that the first Europeans to see it were the British in 1814. Raffles was informed of this discovery and he sent a civil surveyor from Semarang to investigate it. Later he, himself, visited the Borobudur, and the Prambanan, a Hindu temple situated in the same area. When Raffles saw these two remarkable structures, he was thrilled at their antiquity, and at the beauty and delicate execution of the separate portions, the symmetry and regularity of the whole.

But what is most astounding about the Borobudur, is that it was constructed at all. The mere physical labour that was involved is beyond belief. It is estimated that 5,500 cubic metres of stone had to be brought into position, and more than 2,500 square metres of relievos had to be carved. Some thousands of craftsmen had to work for thirty-five years to construct this edifice.

And construct a major work of art they did, one that has not been surpassed anywhere in the world. An eminent art critic has described the relievos as, "The greatest masterpieces of human art, delicate and sensitive in their observation of nature, yet idealized in the beauty and perfection of all creatures."

What kind of a society existed at that time, which enabled men to erect such a tremendous and awe-inspiring structure? One thing is certain, a primitive people ruled by chieftains could not have produced such an edifice.

And this was precisely the point made by a young and earnest Indonesian professor of Archaeology whom we heard lecture on the Borobudur. His main thesis was that the Borobudur represented the logical outgrowth of Javanese civilization, and not merely the result of contact with Indian culture.

He explained that during the rule of the Sailendra kings who were in power from the seventh to the eleventh centuries, a well-organized society already existed in Java. The government hierarchy was complex and very efficient. Taxes were collected and payment in coins was common. Many sacred structures were built. To do this the kings had to marshal an enormous working force. From where did this labour come?

The young professor suggested two possibilities: the workmen employed in building the Borobudur may have been slaves, who had been conquered in war and were then brought to Java, or they may have been peasants from the area who were forced to give a certain amount of free labour to the kings. There was some evidence that peasants built this structure, because after the Borobudur was built, many farmers left Central Java, presumably because the impositions made upon them by the kings were too heavy.

The professor also pointed out that in ancient days the Javanese buried their dead in megalithic structures that were the prototype of the Borobudur. It was common in ancient Java for the relics of the king to be put in a tomb where they could be worshipped by the people. From this evidence, he concluded that the Borobudur must be considered as an indigenous product of Indonesian art and culture.

When he finished speaking, an American lady arose, and in a flat, mid-western drawl said:

"Now, I have been in Indonesia for only a month, and I visited the place you are talking about, and what I would like to find out from you is, what happened to the heads?"

The young man looked at her blankly and repeated: "The heads?"

"Yes, that's right, the heads. You know, the missing heads."

"What missing heads?"

The lady hesitated for a moment, obviously attempting to find a way of expressing herself more clearly. Then she said: "I will try to explain. At this place you talked about—well, the same man is seated everywhere and sometimes he doesn't have a head. And I thought you might be able to tell me what has happened to his head, or perhaps I should say, what has happened to his heads?"

By this time everyone in the audience was in hysterics and the merriment was so infectious that even the dignitaries who had come to the lecture were laughing.

But the lady and the professor remained absolutely serious. Then the professor rubbed his hands together while he muttered: "The heads, the heads."

Then suddenly he said: "I believe I have grasped your question. At the Borobudur there are many images of the Buddha. Some of these images are headless and you are wondering what has happened to those heads."

"You have hit the nail on the head," she said, and at this unpremeditated pun, the audience roared with delight.

The professor was silent until the uproar subsided and then he asked: "Njonja, are you sure you want to know what has happened to the missing heads?"

"Of course I'm sure. If I didn't want to know I wouldn't have taken up all this time."

The young man, looking more earnest than ever, nodded his head. "All right, I will tell you. Borobudur is one of the most beautiful examples of classic Buddhist art in the whole world, and the heads of the Buddha represent sculpture which is so sublime, it is hard to believe that it was done by ordinary men. These heads of the Buddha are priceless art treasures.

"Then why are they missing? Because we were a colony, and we had no way of protecting our artistic heritage, so that many of the heads of the Buddha were taken away from Indonesia, and were sold either to private art collectors, or to museums. For example, when the king of Siam visited Java in 1896, the Dutch Governor-General, C. H. J. van der Wijck, presented him with one of the heads from Borobudur. The most famous Buddhist figure in the world, which was found in Singosari, a town in East Java, is now in the Leyden museum. Similarly,

The sinuous, winding rice terraces of Bali

(*Above*) Sculptured head of a girl in the Hindu Museum, Trawulen

(*Left*) Elaborate inscription on the head stone of the grave of Ibrahim Malik, one of the first holy men to expound the doctrine of Islam in Indonesia

(*Below*) Part of a Buddhist bas-relief at Borobudur depicting musicians and dancing girls

many of the missing heads are exhibited in museums of Amsterdam, Paris, London, and if you will forgive me for saying so, Boston."

"Oh, I do forgive you," she said. "But you must understand I am from Ohio, so I am not responsible for what goes on in Massachusetts, but I can promise you, that when I go home, if I find any of those missing heads in my State, I will do everything in my power to see that they are sent back to you."

"Thank you, Njonja," he said, evidently moved by her sincerity. "I hope that some day all of the missing heads will be returned."

We were surprised at the intensity of his feeling, but later when we went to the Education Conference at Bandung, and learned something about the position of the intellectuals under the Dutch, the reason for his emotional outburst became evident.

Chapter Thirteen

BANDUNG HAD NEVER looked lovelier, but while the Education Conference was in progress we did not have time to leave our hotel where the meetings were taking place. The Conference dealt with three aspects of education; primary schooling; problems at the university level, and means of achieving literacy among the adult population. All of these questions were related to the history of education in Indonesia, which like a turbulent river has many tributaries.

During the Hindu-Javanese period, only the sons of the two highest castes, the Brahmans and the Kshatriyas, received education. But even during that era, there was no formal schooling as we know it today. "The teaching method," one of the Conference speakers pointed out, "was almost the same as in any ancient country, namely: explanation, memorization and recitation. This pattern of memorization, evident in our schools today, had its roots in the very early period of education in Indonesia."

When, in the fifteenth century, Hindu influence was replaced by that of Islam, education was extended to the merchant class, but this education also relied heavily upon memorization of religious texts. However, neither the Hindu nor the Muslim periods affected the lives of the villagers. Dynasties came and went; religions changed; palace intrigues took place, but in the countryside the influential elements were the wind and the rain; the sun and the moon. Nothing disturbed the rhythm of nature; nothing altered the simple economy based on the needs of the individual household or the practical education handed down from father to son, from mother to daughter. As in all other Asian countries, the structure of the economic elements of society remained untouched by the storm clouds of the political sky.

But when the Dutch East India Company and then the Netherlands Government extended its rule over all of the Archipelago, then and then only was the whole static agrarian society shaken to its very foundation and altered once and for all time.

Up until 1848, the Dutch had little interest in educating the Indonesians. Even missionary schools were few in number. But after 1848, the Netherlands Government, bowing to the liberal wind that swept all of Europe, inserted in its new Constitution an article to the effect that, "the Governor-General of the Indies has the responsibility of sponsoring schools for non-Christian children."

Commenting on this, the head of the research division of the Department of Education, declared: "The result of this was that for the first time in colonial history there was an allotment of twenty-five thousand guilders in the budget, to be used for the schooling of non-Christian Indonesians. It was not the amount of money that made this moment notable in the history of Indonesian education, because everyone can imagine what could be done with such a small amount of money, but it was the fact that the colonial government recognized its responsibility for the formal schooling of Indonesian children."

The first schools established under this act were opened only to the children of the aristocrats. In West Java, these schools were called Sekolah Menak, and in Sumatra, Sekolah Radja, meaning schools for the nobility. The education given to this class had a profound effect on the course of the nation's political development, for unlike the Rajas in India who used their education to enforce British rule, many of the sons and daughters of the Radens of Indonesia became nationalist leaders. The Father of Indonesian Nationalism, and the guru of President Sukarno, was Raden Tjokroaminoto; just as the first woman to plead for education of girls, R. A. Kartini, was the daughter of the Regent of Djepara.

But the aristocracy represented only a fragment of the total population.

Almost a century after the reforms of 1848, education was still limited to the wealthy and aristocratic families. In the late 1930s, only two million of the ten million children in the six to fourteen years age group were in school. Because of the lack of primary education further progress was difficult and it was made even more so because only those children acquainted with the use of the Dutch language could pursue a secondary education or go to an institution of higher learning.

There were only forty-two junior high schools with an attendance of 12,000, and in the seventeen senior high schools there were less than 2,500 students. In all of Indonesia there was one university, established only in 1940. It comprised six colleges; medicine and literature in Djakarta; agriculture in Bogor; dental surgery in Surabaja and engineering in Bandung. These six colleges had seventeen hundred students and forty-two professors; of the latter only two were Indonesian.

If students from other islands wished to attend university, they had to come to Java. And if students wished to go abroad, they had to go to Holland. At the elementary level the curriculum was based on the principle of concordancy with the schools in the Netherlands. The Indonesian student had to memorize every creek and village in the Netherlands. At the higher level, the objective of education during the Dutch period was directed not towards the achievement of men capable and reliable, but towards men capable and obedient.

Commenting on the legacy that the Dutch Colonial Government left to the new Republic, the Secretary-General of the Education Ministry, M. Hutasoit, told the Conference:

"In 1945, after three hundred and fifty years of colonial domination, ninety-three per cent of the people were illiterate. There were only a hundred Indonesian physicians; less than a hundred Indonesian engineers; and in a nation dependent upon the efficiency of its land productivity, there were only ten Indonesian agricultural experts."

When the Indonesian Government came to power, it provided in the 1945 Constitution that every citizen is entitled to an education. This right to obtain an education stirred the people far beyond the expectations of the government officials. No one had really evaluated correctly the deep longing that the Indonesians had for education; a privilege denied them for so many years. The people were hungry for schooling; thirsty for knowledge; and so the inexperienced government found itself swamped with demands for primary, secondary and university education.

Everyone wanted to go to school. The ordinary people believed that education would protect them from evil and help to remedy all ills. In the United States, a hundred years before, the working people felt the same way. A group of mechanics meeting in Pennsylvania declared that, "Education is necessary to enable us to raise us from that state of ignorance and poverty, and consequently of vice and wretchedness and woe, to which we have been degraded by the subtle and deceitful machinations of the crafty and wicked."

In the 1840s, a meeting of the Carpenters' Union in New Jersey passed this resolution: "Education alone and that generally diffused is the only prop that will support the fabric of democracy from being crushed beneath the weight of a monopolized and monied aristocracy."

Indonesia, emerging from a period of turbulence heard the same cry. The words of those men and women in the United States, who had proclaimed that, "Only by procuring for all children in the nation free education would working men be able to preserve the Republic from the dangers of foreign invasion and domestic infringement," were echoed a century later in the Indonesian Education Act of 1950, which declared: "For the unity of the people, the Government supplies the need of general education based on the intensification of the national consciousness."

After independence, most of the Dutch teachers returned to Holland. To make up for this, primary schoolteachers were asked to work in secondary schools, and those who had been teaching in the secondary schools became university instructors; while young men and women with only a smattering of learning were mobilized to teach the elementary schoolchildren. At the same time normal schools were created. This project was so successful that today there are more than 200,000 trained teachers.

School buildings were erected through "gotong rojong" or collective effort by the whole community for a common goal. The women's organizations were particularly active in this programme. One of my friends, who belonged to the Kongres Wanita Indonesia, asked if I would save all my empty bottles for her. She explained that with the proceeds from the sale of bottles, her organization planned to build a primary school in a village near Surabaja. I was amazed some months later when she took me to see the school, which was a modern building with good facilities.

There are now more than eight million children in primary schools. Over four hundred junior high schools have been opened with 5,000 teachers and 154,000 students. In the senior high schools there are 800 teachers and 30,000 students. Moreover these schools are located on all the main islands, not only on Java.

But, if the elementary and secondary schools are the foundation of education, the universities are its stars. Since independence seven new universities, comprising forty-two faculties with an enrolment of more than 30,000 students, have been established. The most famous of these are Gadjah Mada in Jogjakarta and Airlangga in Surabaja.

According to its statute which was formulated in the revolutionary days, the University of Gadjah Mada, as a national university, is based on the Pantja Sila—the five principles of which are: Belief in God; Humanity; Social Justice; National Consciousness and Democracy.

Named after the Prime Minister of the Madjapahit Empire, the University has more than 12,000 students. Those studying law, economy and political science, hear lectures in what was once the glamorous ballroom of the Sultan's palace, for he gave this part of the kraton to the University.

In Surabaja, the Airlangga University is named after King Airlangga, who, like President Sukarno was part Balinese and part Javanese. He ruled in the tenth century, uniting Bali and Java. After thirty years he abandoned his throne, and in true Hindu fashion went with his guru into the woods seeking truth and absolution. Because of his god-like ways, it is said that Airlangga was the re-incarnation of the all-powerful Hindu God, Shiva. So the symbol of the Airlangga University shows the King riding on a Garuda, while beneath his feet a snake guards a jar containing the elixir of life—which is knowledge.

The President of Airlangga University is A. G. Pringgodigdo, whose father was the Regent of Tuban. Rather than spend a life in the pursuit of pleasure, although he is a man who enjoys pleasure, he determined to become an administrator. And so he went to Holland where he studied law. When he returned to Java he became an outstanding administrator. One of his Dutch colleagues said to him: "You are the kind of man we would be proud to have as a citizen of our country. Why don't you become a Dutch citizen?" To this, Pringgodigdo replied: "If you are ready to confer Dutch citizenship on every Indonesian, then I, too, will accept the offer. But until that day comes, I shall remain an Indonesian."

After the revolution, Pringgodigdo was appointed as a legal adviser to the Interim Government in Jogjakarta. Later, he became Dean of the Law School and then the first President of Airlangga University in 1954. Besides the three colleges in Surabaja that are affiliated to the University, there is the Faculty of Education in Malang, a lovely city about two hours' drive from Surabaja; and the Udayana Literary Faculty in Denpasar, Bali, which was formally opened in 1959.

In addition to the seven universities, there are also fifteen State Academies with 2,000 students, and twenty-seven private institutions of higher learning with more than 3,000 students.

The teaching staff at the university level is almost all Indonesian, except for a few foreign professors who have been invited to come and teach. The sixty-four Indonesian professors are hard pressed because they must teach at many different faculties. In order to keep on schedule they go by plane from one college to another and as these colleges are located on different islands, it involves quite a bit of travelling. Because of this the students call the professors the "flying gurus". But such levity where a professor is concerned is rare, because the professor enjoys an exalted status.

Like his Dutch predecessor, he occupies the same high position. Independence, nationalism, guided democracy, all bow before him. The professor stands alone at the head of the department. There are no associate or assistant professors. Sometimes students act as assistants and they superintend the practical work while the professor gives the lectures and the examinations, which are the be-all and end-all of the course. One of the foreign experts attending the Conference asked: "How is a professor appointed?" An official of the Ministry of Education answered: "First, the tentative appointee must be approved by the Faculty; then by the Senate of the University and the University President; then the papers are sent to the Cabinet in Djakarta and only when Sukarno himself has signed the request, is the professor appointed."

Not satisfied with having asked this complicated question, the foreign expert stood up again and asked: "How do you get rid of a professor?" There was stunned silence. Get rid of a professor; it was easier for the French to get rid of Louis XVI. After a long pause, the Secretary-General of the Ministry accepted the challenge and replied: "If a professor is not competent, the only way we can get rid of him is by appointing him to a higher position in the Ministry of Education."

To this the foreign expert replied, amidst loud laughter: "That particular system is not unknown to us either."

On this note the Conference was adjourned for the day.

The following morning when the session started it was very lively. For some reason, laymen are always interested in medical problems. In Indonesia, where there are only fifteen hundred physicians to serve the entire community of close to ninety million people, the question of medical training is of the utmost urgency.

When the Dutch first came to the Indies, they fell victim to the same deleterious illnesses as the Indonesians. In fact, they were more incapacitated as they were not accustomed to the tropical climate. They lived in the same way as they had at home. Believing the night air to be a source of illness, they closed every window, and once in bed encircled themselves with pillows, including what has now become known as a Dutch wife. This is a long, round, sausage-like pillow that is found on every bed in Indonesia. Once, when a Javanese went to visit Thailand, he was disconcerted not to find such a pillow on his bed. And so he called the room clerk and asked for a Dutch wife. To which the clerk replied: "I can assure you, sir, Thai wives are much better."

Unlike the Indonesians who bathed many times a day in the river, the Dutch settlers thought of bathing as a way to die young. When the commander of one of the garrisons passed a rule to the effect that his soldiers must bathe, it was countermanded by the Government which forbade forcing the soldiers of the garrison to take a bath once a week.

The Dutch settlers also made the mistake of digging canals, for the canals became pest-holes of infection. One year after a canal was dug near Batavia, hundreds of Dutch citizens became ill and died, perhaps from malaria, possibly from cholera. In the 1770s, when Captain Cook was in Batavia he wrote: "Death means nothing here. The only comment on the death of a fellow citizen is: well, he owed me nothing, or I must get my money from his executors."

The one preventive in which everyone believed was gin. But as the situation changed, though gin remained popular, higher standards of living and improved medical care lowered the mortality rate for the Dutch settlers in Indonesia. During the nineteenth century many Dutch families moved to the hills where the climate was much healthier. Doctors came from the Netherlands to look after their welfare. Sanitation was improved in the Dutch section of the towns. By the beginning of the twentieth century, the average death rate for Europeans in cities of Indonesia was generally only slightly higher than in the towns of Europe.

But among the Indonesians, health standards deteriorated. The move to the cities was hazardous for them because they lived in slum districts. Over-crowding and malnutrition lowered their ability to withstand serious illness. Lack of sanitation increased insect-born, food-born and water-born diseases. Those who remained in the villages were not much better off for they suffered from malaria, filariasis and yaws. But it was the plantation workers who were the most tragic victims of indifference and neglect, and it was this group which had the highest mortality rate from tuberculosis.

During the Japanese occupation the health of the people was at the lowest ebb in the history of the country. There was very little food. Hours of work were increased. All medical supplies were requisitioned for the Japanese armies. And the Japanese went out of their way to persecute doctors, believing them to be the intellectual leaders of the resistance movement. When one of our medical friends incurred the wrath of a Japanese officer, he was saved only because the commander interfered and shouted at his subordinate: "Be careful, you fool. He is the only venereal disease specialist on the island of Sumatra."

After independence, the Government had to cope with many serious and difficult problems in the field of public health. For all practical purposes there were no doctors, nurses, pharmacists, analysts or trained midwives. In addition, because of the terrible years of the Japanese rule, the nutritional status of the people was unsatisfactory, thus affecting the maternity and infant mortality rate as well as resistance to common diseases.

The Government began building new hospitals and expanding the facilities of those already in existence. In co-operation with the World Health Organization, a campaign against malaria, an endemic disease which caused illness among thirty million Indonesians every year, was organized. A similar campaign against yaws was undertaken. To meet the need for additional doctors, the Ministry of Education established new medical schools in Jogjakarta and Surabaja, and for the first time on the islands of Sumatra and Sulawesi.

Gradually, there was a notable rise in the number of medical students. At the Fakultas Kedokteran in Surabaja, there were five graduates in 1951-2, six in 1953-4; twenty-five in 1956-7; and forty-eight in 1957-8. The total enrolment in 1959 was 1,500 students.

At the medical college in Djakarta, one of the faculties of the University of Indonesia, an affiliation was arranged in 1954 with the University of California. One of the changes instituted by the California team was a careful selection of the students admitted, in order to prevent the large number of failures which occurred among the first-, second- and third-year students. After independence any graduate of a high school was permitted to enter the university. Although a very democratic rule, this soon led to confusion, especially in the medical colleges, where tremendous classes and uneven standards of scholarship made teaching difficult.

The California team also shortened the curriculum; increased the amount of practical work in the laboratory and clinic; and made examinations compulsory at the end of the term. In Indonesia, following the Dutch pattern, students are permitted to put off examinations until they feel prepared. In 1959, ninety-seven students, including twenty-one women graduated as the first class that had been brought up under the affiliation, and by far the largest single group to graduate at one time from the medical college.

Describing the graduation ceremony to the Conference, one of the speakers said that each student took an oath, similar to the Hippocratic oath, promising not to divulge any secrets they might learn from their patients. The Christians swore by putting their right hand on the Bible. The Muslims stood under the Koran, which was held overhead by a religious teacher. The Hindu-Balinese students were garlanded and sprinkled with holy water by a Brahman priest. But the "free-thinkers", only promised.

The afternoon session was devoted to a discussion of mass education. The first attempt was made in 1908 by a physician from Jogjakarta, Dr. Wahidin Sudirohusodo, who believed that only through mass education could the Indonesians reach a state comparable to that of the Japanese. Like many intellectuals, he was greatly influenced by the defeat the Russians suffered at the hands of the Japanese in 1905. This event had tremendous repercussions throughout Asia, for it was the first time that the superiority of the white man had been successfully challenged.

Dr. Wahidin toured all of Java, urging every educated person to take an active part in teaching others. As a result of his efforts, the "Budi Utomo", which means seeking perfection, came into being on the twentieth of May, which is celebrated as the Day of National Awakening. We had seen a parade in Surabaja on that occasion. Hundreds of high school boys and girls, dressed in white and riding bicycles took part in the procession.

The cycles were formed into brigades and each group had chosen a special flower as its emblem. The girls wore this flower in their hair, and also decorated the wheels and handlebars of their cycles with the same flowers. So there was the Rose Brigade; the African Daisy Brigade; the Aster Brigade and the Carnation Brigade. Following the cycles, were an equal number of betjaks decorated with flags and banners. The betjak drivers, thin and poorly dressed, were in singular contrast to the girls, who were radiant with youth and beauty. Life, which had dealt harshly with the betjak drivers, had barely touched the girls. It was interesting to see this friendship between the students and the working people which had been initiated by the Budi Utomo movement.

Another stimulus to mass education came from Raden Mas Suwardi

Surjaningrat, of the royal house of Paku Alam. Forced to curtail his nationalist activities, he went to Holland where he studied educational methods. When he returned he started a number of schools known as "Taman Siswa", the student's garden. These schools, like Tagore's Shantiniketan in Bengal, represented an attempt to blend the science of the west with the culture of the east. By 1940, there were more than two hundred and fifty such schools located on the main islands. They were banned during the Japanese occupation.

After independence, the seeds sown by Dr. Wahidin and Raden Mas Suwardi prospered. Today, as a result of the effort of the women's organizations and the Government, more than fifty per cent of the Indonesian people can read and write. One of our Indian friends, a weaving master in the Government factory producing sugar bags from Rosella, a plant resembling jute, was amazed when he found that every worker there could sign his name. In the jute factory in Bengal, where he had worked before, less than a hundred of his two thousand employees could do this; all the rest used thumb prints as identification marks.

One of the main reasons why literacy has become so widespread in such a short time is that Bahasa Indonesia can be learned quickly and easily. As one of the members of the Education Conference pointed out, Bahasa Indonesia is phonetic, written in Latin script and employs only twenty-one letters. Although it has always been a medium of speech among the traders of Malaya and Indonesia, the language did not come into popular use until the time of the Japanese invasion. Having banned Dutch, the Japanese found it impossible to substitute their own language. So, for purely selfish reasons they encouraged the use of Bahasa Indonesia. This in turn, helped to forge a bond of unity among the people living on different islands, as before that time most of them spoke only their mother tongue, such as Javanese, Sundanese, Madurese, Sumatran, Balinese, etc.

Bahasa Indonesia is a growing language. Without hesitation, words are borrowed from Arabic, Sanscrit, Urdu, Javanese, Dutch, Portuguese and English. Because of the progress the language has made in Indonesia, the Government of Malaya decided to change the Malayan script from Arabic to Latin; to accept those words which have been incorporated into Bahasa and to obtain instructors in the language from Indonesia.

Grammatically uncomplicated, Indonesian has neither tenses nor genders. It is pronounced as written with few exceptions. The "dj" is pronounced as a "j" in English; the "tj" is like "ch"; and "j" is pronounced like "y". That is the reason Djakarta is sometimes spelled Jakarta; Tjirebon as Cheribon; and Surabaja as Surabaya.

The most amusing aspect of Bahasa is that instead of adding an "s" to make the plural, the word is repeated. Thus, a child is an "anak" and children are "anak-anak". Since this looks clumsy in print, it is written "anak²", so that all over the newspapers there are literally hundreds of twos.

Most pleasant for foreigners is the ease with which they can learn the language so that many attending the conference had a working knowledge of Bahasa. For this reason the closing speech was made in Indonesian. The speaker used as his theme the inaugural address made by President Sukarno at the opening of the Udayana Literary Faculty in Bali. At the time, the President, alluding to the period when Airlangga was in power, declared: "We must wake up the people and tell them we have a glorious past; we must make them realize the significance of our current struggle and finally, we must convince them that we will have a bright future."

Chapter Fourteen

ONE LOVELY COOL DAY during the winter month of July, 1959, a physician from Bali, who was interested in pharmacology, visited my husband at his office in the Fakultas Kedokteran. Later, he and his princess-wife came to our house. She was a tiny, languorous beauty with a splendid figure and soft Polynesian features that might have been painted by Gauguin. While we were having tea, she said, in charming but stilted English: "I do hope that you will be able to come to Bali next month and attend the cremation of my grandfather."

"I am so sorry to hear about your grandfather," I answered feeling that some polite rejoinder was necessary.

"There is no need for you to be sorry," she replied. "Grandfather has been dead for twenty-five years, and it is only now that we can afford to have him cremated."

"Do you mind if I ask where he has been all these years?"

"Buried, of course," she answered. "But being buried is only a temporary state. Every Balinese must be cremated. Only then can the soul of the departed be purified and liberated. As we belong to a noble family, we have to make provision for some of his friends as well. We would not like him to be alone when he starts on his last journey, the final stage before reincarnation."

"How many friends will accompany him?" I asked.

"Thirty-four."

"That should be quite enough."

"It is enough," the princess agreed, "but not nearly as many as would have accompanied a man like my grandfather in the old days. Then a person of his eminence would have had at least a hundred companions. It is too bad that we are not as well off as our ancestors," she added, sighing.

"But why is the cremation so expensive?" I inquired. "In India, among the Hindus it is a simple affair and does not involve a great deal of money."

"You must not compare India with Bali, for they are very different," the husband of the princess replied. He was an attractive man, but western dress could not conceal that softness and delicacy which is characteristic of Balinese, men as well as women. Dark eyes; long, sweeping lashes; a well-formed nose; and heart-shaped lips over pearly white teeth that had obviously been filed to form a straight line; all set within the framework of a round, beardless face, made him appear like a youth, although his age must have been at least forty.

"Many people," he declared, "who do not know much about Bali assume that its culture is very much like that of India. Superficially that is so, because we are also Hindus. But basically, because of certain geographic, racial and historic factors, our Hinduism has developed in its own fashion.

"The people of Bali are almost all rice farmers who work hard for a living, but they have never been subject to starvation or extreme poverty. Nature has been unbelievably generous and bountiful to Bali. So wonderful does a Balinese find his life that he believes when he dies, the first heaven to which he will be allowed entrance before reincarnation, will be exactly like Bali.

"Even our ceremonies are not the same as those practised by Indian Hindus. We do not consider a wedding of special importance, but a fine cremation is an absolute necessity, and the reason it is so expensive," he explained, "is because of the elaborate preparations that must be made beforehand, and the large number of guests who are invited. And because we are a rich Brahman family, we must arrange for the cremation of others from our village."

"But if there is no wealthy family in the village, how can the ordinary Balinese afford such a costly affair?" I asked.

The doctor, still smiling, replied: "That is quite simple. A community ceremony is arranged in which the financial burden is shared by all."

"Is there a special month or day when the cremation must take place?"

"There is," the princess replied, "and the auspicious date is set by the Brahman priest. But he has to take the financial situation of the family into consideration as well."

"What a difficult problem, and what a sad occasion," I murmured, revealing the typical attitude of a westerner towards financial problems and death.

"Not sad at all," the princess corrected me. "On the contrary, it is a day of joy. For on this day, those we love are finally freed from earthly cares."

Having said this, she and her husband rose and asked for permission to take their leave as they had several other calls to make before returning to Bali. Just as they were leaving, the princess said again: "Don't forget, we will be expecting you in our village for the ceremony."

And so in August, we decided to visit Bali: the Magic Isle, the Isle of the Gods, the Isle of Romance, the Enchanted Isle, all extravagant names, but not one rich enough to capture the fascination of that land of golden dreams where two million people live and work, and are incapable of producing anything that is not artistic.

Most tourists going to Bali, either fly from Djakarta to the largest and most important city, Denpasar, or go by ship which lands at the capital city, Singaradja. But we thought it would be more interesting to drive, for then we could follow the route taken by those nobles of Java, who not wishing to become Muslims, had migrated to Bali in the fifteenth century. They took with them their poets, dancers, actors, craftsmen, soldiers and priests, and they systematically preserved their ancient Javanese-Hindu culture. So even today, Bali is a mirror reflection of what life must have been like in Java hundreds of years ago.

The Javanese nobility who fled to Bali belonged to the Kshatriya caste as they were the warriors and rulers. Their scholars and priests were Brahmans, and together they attempted to control the economic and political destiny of the Balinese by introducing the caste system. They designated the ordinary Balinese, who were of Polynesian origin and who constituted ninety per cent of the population, as "sudras", low-caste people. But the Balinese ignored this designation, as long before the advent of the Javanese, they had established their own aristocracy, based on village lineage.

The Javanese rulers also tried to wrest the land away from the collective village control. Many Balinese heroes, such as the romantic Djajaprana, arose to challenge the new aristocracy. But even today the question of land ownership remains unsettled.

Before we left for our vacation on the Magic Isle, we calculated that we would need at least five thousand rupiahs. We took four thousand in thousand rupiah notes and the rest in small bills which could be spent on our drive there. Happily unaware of the dark fiscal future that awaited us, we left Surabaja late in the morning and drove towards Banjunwangi, a small, quaint town on the easternmost tip of Java. There we spent the night in a pension with the high-sounding name Afro-Asian Hotel, and the next morning took the landing-ship that plies back and forth across the two-mile stretch of water that separates the islands.

On the LST there was room for about six cars and thirty people. Although the Bali straits were as smooth as a lake, some of the women and children were sea-sick. The Balinese do not like the sea and consider it the haunt of evil and danger. They avoid crossing any body of water and in the old days Balinese refused to become sailors. The sea, which has always attracted the adventurers of the world, with its promise of new vistas, has never had any lure for the Balinese. They turn their backs on the sea and gaze in reverence at the mountains from whence come all things that are good.

Aboard the LST every sailor was Javanese, except one, a Balinese whose good looks were slightly marred by a split lip. To hide this defect he wore a moustache and a small, pointed beard, made popular in South-East Asia by President Ho Chi-minh. This sailor had especially fine hands which had not been spoiled by his rough sailor's work, and as I watched him moving quickly and gracefully from one part of the little ferry to another, I thought he seemed more like an artist than a sailor.

After an hour and a half we reached Gilimanuk on the Bali side. We had a great deal of trouble getting our car up the soft, black volcanic sand to the road. Finally a rope was tied to the car, and more than twenty men, amidst shouts of laughter as though they were playing a game, succeeded in getting the car across the sand. Much to our surprise, we had to check with the Customs office, a formality which is required when going from one Indonesian island to another.

Our first impression of Bali was disappointing as the terrain was dry and barren. There is little water in the western part of the island and most of the inhabitants are Madurese, not Balinese. Our disappointment turned to chagrin when we hit the first bump, and this was just the beginning, because we had to drive for seventy-two kilometres on a road as rough as a river bed. The only bright moments were when we passed the road workers, lovely Balinese girls wearing large, white garden party hats to protect them from the sun; their long, black hair hanging to their waists.

Just when we were losing hope, we came to a fine paved highway, and within a few moments we were driving through scenery so startling and so magnificent that it did not seem to be real. On one side of us were the mountains, tall, dark, sombre volcanoes. On the other was the Indian Ocean, its huge grey waves pounding the black sand.

Everywhere we looked were rows and rows of sinuous and winding paddy terraces, stretching from the sea to the mountains, and all in different stages of cultivation. The terraces were exactly as that warm-hearted Mexican artist and writer, Miguel Covarrubias, had described them twenty years before: "like flights of gigantic stairs."

Some of the paddy fields had been filled with water and fat, downy ducks floated on the surface. Others had just been transplanted and the young blades of rice were still chartreuse in colour. Where the rice had matured, it looked as though an improvident jeweller had scattered Chinese jade. And where the rice had already been harvested the caked mud was a deep, velvety brown.

There is an ancient fable that the people of Bali did not have rice but only the juice of sugar-cane as food. "Then the male god of fertility and water, Wisnu, came to earth in disguise in order to provide the Balinese with better food. He raped an unwilling Mother Earth to fertilize her and give birth to rice, and she became known as Sanghyang Ibu Pretiwi, the Smitten Grandmother. Then Wisnu made war on Indra, the Lord of the Heavens, to induce him to teach men how to grow rice. Thus, as the principle source of life and wealth and as a gift from the gods, rice was born from the cosmic union of the divine male and female creative forces represented in earth and water."

It is rice that has determined the social organization of Bali. Except where the predatory Javanese nobles, after years of intrigue, succeeded in gaining control of the land, the paddy fields belong to the village; never to the individual. Irrigation facilities are also the property of the village. The Balinese farmers are members of a co-operative society known as the "subak", which has the right to determine the amount of land and water distributed to each cultivator. If the field is not tended carefully, members of the subak may vote to take the land away from that particular farmer and give it to someone else.

Orders given by the subak must be obeyed for they represent the decision of the group. In Bali, even more than in Java, the spirit of "tolong menolong" or "mutual help", dominates the life and work of the people. A villager often gives his labour for the good of the community; in return he receives assistance and protection. This organizational pattern is not confined to agriculture but extends to the arts as well.

In every village there is a large council house, a rectangular structure, supported by bamboo pillars and covered by a thatched roof, but without walls. It is here that matters of village importance are discussed. Near the council house there is a huge gong which is sounded if an emergency arises. Once a month, instead of meeting in the council house, an assembly is held in a shed situated in the middle of the rice field. This small shrine, owned by the subak, is dedicated to the gods who watch over the rice fields. As we drove, we saw many of these tiny, open pavilions with thatched roofs, held up by two living trees, one at each end, their branches extending upwards and outwards, so that the shrine is always protected by this green, leafy shade.

We arrived in Denpasar at sundown, and as we entered the city my husband began driving slower and slower. This puzzled me as he is usually not so concerned with traffic regulations. Then I noticed what had attracted his attention. In front of us there was a bicycle, and seated on it was a young man, pedalling furiously. Just behind him was a beautiful girl, and on her head was a large water jug which she was holding in place with her hand, her right arm curved in an arc above her body. She wore an ankle-length Balinese sarong and that was all. As the cycle sped along the uneven road, her large, full breasts bumped up and down. Totally unaware of the picture she presented, her only interest was in keeping the water jug safely on her head.

Nothing in Denpasar was as impressive as the total absence of betjaks. We were surprised, for in most of the cities of Java, the betjaks comprise the main form of transportation. But here in Denpasar, there was not a single one. Nor did we see any man pulling heavy loads. Later we learned that the Balinese consider it undignified for a human being to do the work of a draft animal, and for that reason betjaks have never been allowed on the island.

We did not stay in the city as we had made arrangements to spend our vacation at the annexe of the Bali Hotel, situated on the beach at Sanur. Arriving there we found a note from our friends, who had written that we should come to their village that very night in order to see the preparations being made for the cremation which was to take place the next day.

Soon after dinner, we drove to the village. It was the night of the full moon. As we wended our way along the edge of the volcanic mountains, the island seemed like a technicolor film. But even a Hollywood producer would hesitate to show a moon as dazzling as the Bali moon; stars as bright as the Bali stars; or sand as black as the Bali sand. Even the most imaginative stage designer would be reluctant to create a set in which sculptured paddy-fields glistened in the moonlight like diamonds set in platinum.

It was not late, but the countryside was already quiet and only the croaking of frogs disturbed the stillness of the night. But when we came within sight of the village, there was as much commotion as if it were the middle of a market day. All of the activity was centred around the temple. In the courtyard there were hundreds of men gambling with dice. It reminded us of the Kasada festival.

Inside the courtyard, we were met by the Balinese physician and his wife. He was in traditional dress which especially suited him. The princess wore a fine batik, and over it a blouse of French lace. Around her slender waist she had tied a wide sash, which is worn whenever the women go to the temple. In her hair there were flowers of gold.

In the centre of this inner court there was a wooden platform, about one storey high, and seated on the top was a Brahman priest. He was chanting in Sanscrit, oblivious to all the noise directly under him, and there was a great deal. For just below the priest, a huge turtle was being teased by the children. The pleasant life of the turtle was coming to an end as he was to be made into soup, which would be served the next day. A large pot of water, set on a charcoal fire, was being prepared for him.

At ten o'clock, the gamelan orchestra began playing, and our host explained that the Wayang Kulit was about to begin. A large screen had been placed at one end of the court, and most of the guests were seated on the ground in front of it. We walked behind the screen, and there we met the master of the Wayang, a lean man, naked to the waist, but wearing a sarong and a Balinese head-dress. He was seated cross-legged, next to the screen. Hanging just at the level of his head was a large oil lamp, really a kettle with a wick in the spout. This was kept burning throughout the performance in order to cast the shadow play on the screen.

The face of the Wayang master, who is called a "dalang", was protected from the heat of the lamp by a sheet of iron that was attached to the lamp and reflected the light towards the screen. Long before the drama began, the master made his preparations. He drank several cups of tea and ate some rice, as he would be working continuously for five or six hours. Then he chewed betel in order to gain more strength. After that he offered prayers to the deities who guide the Wayang Kulit. Finally he opened the mysterious, rectangular wooden box in which the leather puppets were kept.

There were more than two hundred figures lying in the box. Carefully, the dalang took them out, one by one. The puppets were on sharp sticks and the Wayang master placed each stick in the stem of a banana tree which was lying across the foot of the screen. He put the good puppets to his right and the evil ones to his left. But each puppet, good or evil, was as ugly as sin. There are many explanations for this.

The Wayang Kulit had its origin in Central Java, during the Hindu period. At this time, the puppets looked like people. But with the advent of Islam, the Javanese were forbidden to present the Wayang Kulit because the puppets resembled human beings; and such representation is forbidden by the Koran. To circumvent this proscription, the Javanese deformed the figures until they had no resemblance to living things. And when they did this, the orthodox Muslims no longer objected to the performances.

The Wayang Kulit is a drama which represents the constant struggle between the forces of good and the forces of evil. The stories are taken from the *Ramayana* and the *Mahabharata*. But, over the years, Javanese legends have been added and rowdy clowns introduced. The clowns comment on all matters, not excluding the economic condition of the country and the affairs of public persons.

When the performance began, the master took a lacy, gilded leaf and drew it across the screen with a twirling motion, creating a dancing shadow. This meant that the drama was about to begin. When the puppet was a god or a king, the dalang spoke in Sanscrit, but when a clown was on the screen he spoke in Balinese. This enabled the audience to follow the story. Not only did the master use his voice and both hands, but also his right foot, with which he tapped out a curious rhythm, banging a piece of horn against the side of the wooden box which had contained the puppets.

Later, we went in front of the screen and sat on the ground. The grotesque, shadowy puppets, speaking in high, unnatural voices, captivated our attention. The Balinese children as well as the adults were as enchanted as if this were the first time they had seen the performance. I found it interesting that in the middle of the twentieth century, this puppet drama should be able to compete against the ubiquitous cinema.

It was nearly two in the morning when we left the courtyard and the next day we had to start out at seven o'clock. Following the instructions of our host we went to an exquisite Hindu-Balinese temple. Thousands of people were already assembled there. The village women had come bearing wonderful combinations of fruits and flowers, artistically arranged in pyramids on top of bamboo stands.

After a while we heard the sound of the "kulkul". This is a hollowed tree trunk, carved in the shape of a demon, and beaten on all ceremonial occasions. When the last note of the kulkul died away the procession appeared. Hundreds of singing, dancing, cheering men, women and children came towards us, every colour in the rainbow blended in a riotous display. So quickly did the drummers pound that the notes seemed to be tumbling over one another. Flags and banners waved in the breeze. The women, walking like goddesses, carried sacrificial offerings on their heads.

Suddenly we heard loud cries of excitement, the funeral tower was being pulled to the appointed place by hundreds of men. The tower was at least twenty times as tall as the men, and, like a skyscraper, it dominated the entire scene. This edifice was a fantastic creation of wood, tinsel, mirrors, cotton wool and paper flowers. On the back there was an image of Bhoma, the Son of the Earth, with his mouth open, his fangs bared and his wings outstretched as though to encompass the world.

The tower was divided into three symbolic parts. The lower part represented the nether world, that haunted site of demons which among the Balinese is always associated with the sea. The middle part symbolized the world in which we live, where happiness and sorrow meet in an ever-shifting pattern. At this level of the tower, a special platform called the "padmasan" had been constructed to carry the bones which were to be cremated. The upper part of the tower, decorated in vivid colours, created the illusion of the wonderful world hereafter, where there is no pain or suffering but only pleasure and joy.

High above at the very crest of the tower, were the Chinese-like pagodas, always odd in number, signifying the caste of the family. The Sudras may have only one, the Vaisyas three, the Kshatriyas five or seven and the Brahmans nine or eleven. With a great deal of shoving, pulling and tugging the stately tower was finally fixed in the proper place. Soon thereafter a tall, wooden bridge was placed against it. Agile young men climbed the steps and stood along the bridge to form a human chain. Then, one by one, the neatly packaged bones, looking as attractive as Christmas gifts, were taken from the padmasan and handed from one man to the next and finally to the female relatives of the deceased. These women wore white ribbons around their foreheads to distinguish them from the guests.

The packages were brought to the Brahman priest who was standing on the floor of an open shed containing carved wooden animals. It was in these creatures that the remains were placed and finally burned. Brahman bones are put, of course, in the sacred cow, Kshatriya bones in a winged lion, Vaisya bones in a deer and Sudra bones in a fish. Offerings were also placed on the floor of the shed so that the animals stood deep in flowers and fruits.

After these preparations, there was a short interlude while the gamelan played, tea was served, and the Brahman priest did an intricate dance. Then precisely at two o'clock, kerosene was poured over the tower and the flame applied. The beautiful edifice, which had taken weeks of concentrated labour to construct, caught fire immediately, and waves of heat assailed us as the flames quickly spread. The people watched anxiously to see which way the tower would fall. Fortunately it toppled in an auspicious direction, and there was an audible sigh of relief.

Just as the tower was crumbling, the priest set fire to the shed in which the animals were standing. But he did not use kerosene, which is forbidden for such a purpose. Instead he used a piece of bamboo that had been dipped in fat and set on fire with the aid of a magnifying glass held in the sunlight. Soon the cows, lions and deer fell; their painted faces resting on the flowers; their Picasso-like eyes gazing at the clear blue sky. When they were completely consumed the cremation was over. Only the smell of charred cloth and wood filled the air.

Within a few moments the grounds were empty, as though no one had ever been there. The Balinese left to take part in a great feast that was to be held in the village, where they would eat the turtle who had been teased by the children the night before. The tourists hurried away, shaken by the dramatic intensity of the event.

Forty-two days later, there would be another ceremony in which the ashes would be placed in golden urns. These would be carried to the sea-shore and put on small sailing boats which would go far from the shore, so that the souls of those who had departed could not return to the land. This would be the finale. The Balinese believe that their relatives, who have become deities, will always watch over them, with the same loving interest as when they were human beings and lived on the beautiful island of Bali.

When we returned to Denpasar, my husband suddenly stopped the car. There in the window of an art shop, was a painting of a cremation. It was as bold, weird and exciting as the ceremony itself.

Chapter Fifteen

ALTHOUGH we had been impressed by the painting of the cremation, it had not prepared us for the treasure we were to discover when we entered the small art gallery. For there, displayed on the walls were paintings of such beauty and strength that it took our breath away.

During our stay in Surabaja, we had seen many paintings by Indonesian artists, for this is a land where pictures are bought and sold like any ordinary commodity. There are paintings for sale in bookshops; grocery stores; restaurants and bazaars. Along the main street of any sizeable town, original oil-paintings can be bought for less than the price of a pair of shoes. The canvases are generally realistic in style, portraying landscapes, people or animals. They are always carefully painted and nicely framed. Pedlars come to the door hawking these pictures in the same casual way they sell fruit and vegetables. They even go into the kampungs with their wares and are able to find buyers. President Sukarno is not alone in being a collector of paintings. There is hardly a single householder throughout the length of Java who does not own at least one original picture.

But in these canvases we recognized something new and fresh; a dynamic ability to reproduce the essence of human feeling. Seeing us, the artist came over and said, in the only English he knew: "It is all the struggle for life." My husband said that he would like to purchase two paintings and asked the artist, whose name we learned was B. Soegeng, to come to our hotel the following day and bring the pictures. One was of the cremation; the other of a woman, her long hair falling around her shoulders, her eyes closed and her face convulsed with some secret, calamitous sorrow.

Early the next morning, Soegeng appeared, looking every inch an artist, as he wore a bright blue batik shirt and a dark red beret, perched jauntily on his head. We invited him to have coffee with us and as he sat on the veranda of our suite enjoying the brilliance of the sunshine, he told us something about his life. Born in middle Java, the son of an elderly father and a young mother, both of whom were itinerant dancers, neither Soegeng nor his eight brothers and sisters were able to attend school regularly. But all of them became interested in the arts.

Soegeng's own life had been filled with hardship. He drifted from one place to another, always painting and at the same time taking whatever job he could find, so that he would have at least one bowl of rice a day. He had even worked for Indonesia's first Prime Minister. Soetan Sjahrir. But he never stayed in one place very long, because he was determined to devote all of his energy to painting. Finally, he left Java and settled in a Balinese village, where he found the inspiration and the atmosphere he was seeking, but success eluded him as he could not sell his paintings.

"You will understand the reason for this," he told us in Bahasa Indonesia, "when you see examples of Balinese traditional painting and the work being done by the European artists staying here. Perhaps, this afternoon we can drive to Ubud, the art centre of Bali, and visit the museum."

That afternoon, on our way to Ubud, we soon realized that though Soegeng's paintings were serious, he was a gay and flirtatious young man. Whenever we stopped, he greeted the women over twenty-five as "mother" and those under that age as "darling". He seemed to be well known in every village and we had to stop often to meet his friends.

Just before climbing the tree- and flower-studded hill that leads to the Ubud museum, we were stopped by a boy of about eighteen, who wanted to show us his sketches. He had at least a hundred water colours, all in the same traditional Balinese style, reminiscent of the work of Henri Rousseau, but with even greater attention to detail. When we congratulated him on his skill, and agreed to buy one of his water colours, he said, by way of apology:

"I am just earning my living by painting until I can do what I want to do."

We gazed at him in sheer disbelief, for this was certainly a new version of an old story. Every artist we had ever heard of had to do other work in order to paint, and here he was painting "just to earn a living". Unable to contain myself, I asked him what he wanted to do. He replied: "I want to be an army officer. But after the death of my father I was forced to take care of my mother and sisters. The only way I could make enough money was to paint and sell my pictures. But as soon as I have enough, I will chuck this and go into the army."

At this point, Soegeng was laughing so hard that tears had come into his eyes: "You can see," he said, "why this is called the Magic Isle. Is there any place else in the world where you paint for a living while yearning to do something else? And if I were willing to paint in this formal style, I, too, would have plenty of money."

The young boy was quite puzzled by our glee, but he was happy to have sold one of his sketches and so he accompanied us to the door of the Museum. Built with funds donated by the Rockefeller Foundation, it is a splendid, rectangular building of teak and bamboo. The paintings were hung artistically, but we found them disappointing. They were fine examples of classical Balinese art, but like the water colours, they were formal, unemotional and preoccupied with detail.

Later that evening we visited several painters. Some were from Java, a few from Europe and one from America. All of them were intrigued with Bali, but none had been able to grasp its essential character. They romanticized the people and turned the women into cover girls. Nor were their landscapes more successful as most of them looked like photographs. Seeing these paintings, my husband remarked that perhaps the artists had failed because they were surrounded by too much beauty.

But if the traditional painting of Bali seems stiff and formal, the sculpture is strikingly imaginative. This is surprising because Balinese sculpture is also a traditional art, handed down from generation to generation, so one would expect it to be as stylized as the painting. But on the contrary, it is brimming with originality. There are many sculptors scattered throughout the island but the most famous centre for sculpture is in a village called Mas.

My husband, who had studied sculpture with William Zorach in the States, was fascinated by the superb carvings and wanted to buy them all. What delighted him most is the ability of the Balinese to work in so many different media and their adaptability to each one. They use wood, stone, ivory, bone, horn and any other material which comes to hand. The object created always conforms to the quality and shape of the medium chosen. Thus, one of the finest carvings we saw was that of an imaginary bird which had been carved from the gnarled roots of a large tree.

Some of the wood carvings are rough hewn; others highly polished and still others, painted. Although many of the statues represent mythological characters, a few are pure abstractions; interesting shapes in which the artist gives free play to his fancies. The typical Balinese carving is often distorted in order to accentuate the special character of the subject, or to enhance its natural beauty.

Equally interesting is the complete absence of any inhibitions. The Balinese, like the ancient Hindus, do not resort to camouflage but present sex in an open and free fashion, yet untainted by any vulgarity. There are carvings depicting a bird laying an egg; an animal nursing its young or embracing its mate. The sculptors do not employ phallic symbols, because in their carvings the sex organs are clearly delineated, even exaggerated. The potency of the male is an important factor in Balinese mythology as well as in all the other arts, particularly the dance.

Our friend Soegeng was a devotee of the dance, not to mention the dancers, and he insisted that we go with him to see performances in different villages. He told us that the Balinese never praise an individual performer, but reserve their compliments for the village. Thus a true Balinese will say: "In my village we have the best Oleg dancers, but in my brother-in-law's village, one can see the finest Barong."

Each village vies with the others to produce the finest musicians and dancers. These artists lead a dual life. In the daytime they must work for a living, and it is only when the sun sets that they don the royal robes of the theatre. Because of this, there is a fusion of work and art which is unique. Men who toil in the paddy fields during the day, will enchant the tourists at night by their polished performances. Waiters in the hotels become musicians at night. Children of ordinary cultivators are transformed into ballerinas. When they go abroad they astonish audiences with their professional talent. In Bali, there are no amateurs; there are only professionals. And there is no folk art as distinguished from professional art.

While most dance performances are held at night, the Barong is given during the daylight hours. So one morning we drove with Soegeng to a village near Denpasar where this dance drama was being performed. When we arrived at the temple grounds, members of the gamelan orchestra were already assembled; handsome young men, dressed in hand-woven sarongs, spotless white shirts, and wearing the Bali male head-dress, a Batik square which is tied and worn in such a way as to disclose the character of the individual. The instruments were arranged in rows, and the men seated cross-legged behind them. Suddenly the leader sounded the opening note and this was followed by a loud, sustained crash; a sound at once startling and exquisite and so high pitched that it was difficult to catch the melody.

The orchestra played for a few moments, and then from the temple entrance, for all Balinese dances take place in front of the temple, there appeared a figure of such imaginative concept as to delight the most sophisticated tourist. This ugly, clumsy creature with popping eyes and a small snapping mouth; long white hair dotted with jewels; a pompous golden tail that swished as he romped—was the Barong, a friend of man.

The Barong's most formidable enemy is the Rangda, powerful and cruel queen of the witches who has been endowed with the secrets of black magic. The clash between the Barong and the Rangda is an eternal one, signifying the same basic conflict between good and evil which was depicted in the Wayang Kulit. The Rangda made her entrance on the shoulders of a slave; her dishevelled hair reaching to her feet and her long tongue ending in a flame.

Carrying the brunt of the performance were the young girl dancers who took the parts of the maidservants, the prince and the princess. Ranging in age from eight to twelve, they thrilled the spectators with the brilliance of their technique. Dressed in gorgeous costumes of brocade, and wearing gold-painted crowns ornamented with fresh frangipani flowers, they had the self-confidence, the grace and elegance that comes from disciplined training.

These children, like Indian brides, had white dots painted on their foreheads just above the eyebrows. Their eyes and lashes were heavily made up, for in Balinese dance, the face remains impassive and only the movement of the eyes reveals the secret of the character who is being portrayed. The eyes of the children expressed every mood, ranging from fear to joy, their long, blackened lashes fluttering against their pale cheeks like swift, small birds.

They were equally skilful with their hands and fingers, which were as supple as though they were boneless. They executed complicated hand gestures; the movements being part of the sign language of the dance used to evoke images and emotions.

The climax of the drama came when the followers of the Barong decided to attack the Rangda. At the sound of a certain note, the male dancers, each with kris in hand, rushed after the witch. But by joining the thumbs of her outstretched hands and yelling a curse, she succeeded in turning every kris against its owner. The Barong, realizing that his supporters were in danger, called upon his magic power to protect them by hardening their skin so that the kris could not penetrate.

At this point the dance became wild, as the dancers had fallen into a trance. Each one was trying to force the pointed blade of the kris into his body. Even when the music stopped the dancers continued their frenzied acrobatics, and it was not until the Brahman priest sprinkled water on each dancer that some of them, but not all, came out of the trance. Thus "evil" had triumphed but "good" still lived to fight another day.

Most Balinese dances combine the esoteric influence of the temple and the worldly influence of the court. They are finished products that have been polished for hundreds of years. But they also represent experimentation, for the Balinese dancers do not hesitate to blend traditional and modern concepts, and are constantly introducing innovations. In the entire repertoire of Balinese dance, there is only one which might be considered as primitive and that is the famous "Ketjak" dance drama which is performed either by the villagers of Bona or Bedulu.

One evening we drove to Bedulu, passing over many narrow bridges that span deep ravines. In the rivers far below, men and women were bathing; the women on one side, the men on the other. Their laughter drifted up to us like a soft cloud of smoke. At Bedulu a huge crowd had collected—tourists, villagers and babies. Many of the babies had their heads completely shaved except for one appealing lock of hair which fell over the forehead and often served to hold a flower blossom.

When it became completely dark, a huge oil lamp was lit and soon thereafter a hundred and fifty men appeared. They were barefoot and wore only short loin cloths. Each man had placed a brilliant red hibiscus flower behind his right ear. After a few moments, they all sat down, forming five or six concentric circles. There was absolute silence as the Brahman priest blessed them, and then, suddenly, as an arrow is shot from a bow, the men sat up very straight and began uttering the sharp cry that was to punctuate the dance like the rat-a-tat-tat of a machine-gun—"ketjak—ketjak—ketjak".

No one really knows the history of this strange and powerful dance, performed only by men. It is the most virile of all Balinese dances, devoid of any softness or femininity. It is thought that during the period when animism was practised, it served as an accompaniment to a trance dance of virgins, who, like the Oracle of Delphi, were able to repeat the wishes of the gods.

While it lasts, the dance has a hypnotic effect. One feels caught in the tumultuous sway of a hundred and fifty men shouting, sometimes softly, sometimes loudly—"ketjak—ketjak—ketjak". When it is over the absence of this sound is devastating. The cry rang in our ears until it was driven away by the natural sounds of men, talking, laughing and bidding each other good night. The dancers, who seemed to have been possessed with supernatural power, were only ordinary human beings. And many of them carried their farm implements with them, when they left the scene of the dance.

The next morning, while walking through the village, we suddenly heard the ketjak call again. Then we noticed a group of little boys, seated in concentric circles, practising the ketjak dance. The leader was not more than eight years old, but he was very strict and if anyone made a mistake, the group had to repeat that part of the dance. When the boys saw us they began giggling, but the leader soon put an end to such foolishness, and the boys continued to practise. From this demonstration we realized how the tradition of Balinese dance is carried on from one generation to the next.

More than two decades ago, Miguel Covarrubias wondered whether Balinese art would be destroyed as the outside world made its effect felt on the people of the island. He particularly feared the increasing number of tourists and the advent of modern technology. But his fears were groundless. Despite the sweeping changes that have taken place in Indonesia and in Bali during the intervening years, the rich and dynamic culture of the island has neither been spoiled nor corrupted. That is because all art in Bali stems from the people and belongs to them. There is no separation between the social, economic, religious and artistic aspects of life. Unlike the west, artists do not constitute a separate, pampered entity. Dancers, musicians, painters and sculptors are firmly integrated in village life, and it is from the village that they seek their inspiration.

Many foreigners think of the Balinese as imaginative dreamers who have never been concerned with the mundane affairs of state, and are blissfully unaware of political forces. This concept is as naïve as it is inaccurate, for the Balinese have always been staunch nationalists. Among the Dutch, they had a reputation of being fierce and war-like. For that reason, and because Bali was not tempting economically, the Dutch did not try to conquer the island until the end of the nineteenth century. Then, taking advantage of a quarrel that had arisen between one of the Bali kings and the Raja who ruled the adjacent island of Lombok, the Dutch intervened. In Lombok, they encountered fanatic resistance which they succeeded in subduing. The Raja of Lombok was exiled to Java. At the same time the Dutch had gained a foothold in northern Bali.

Their next opportunity occurred in 1904, when a small Chinese steamer was wrecked on the beach at Sanur. The ship was looted and the owner held the Dutch Government responsible for his losses. He demanded compensation. The Dutch tried to get this from the Raja of Badung, who refused. Angered by his peremptory refusal, the Dutch dispatched a military expedition to Bali, which landed at Sanur Beach. There the ships' cannons opened fire on the palace and the commanding officer ordered the Raja to surrender.

Unwilling to become a captive of the Dutch, the Raja, followed by his wives, children and courtiers, all of whom were clad in white and armed with spears, advanced towards the enemy. The Dutch soldiers were stunned seeing this apparition, for the women had let their hair down; the children wore jewellery; the krises of the Raja's guards, with their handles of pure gold embedded with rubies and diamonds, glittered in the sun. The Raja's party continued to advance and then fell upon the Dutch soldiers, attacking without mercy. Their commander ordered them to fire, and soon the field was covered with bodies. This battle was called the "puputan",—a fight to the finish.

By 1914, the Dutch had managed to occupy all of Bali, but their tenure on the island was so uncertain and attacks against them so savage, that they were forced to maintain a large garrison there until the late 1930s. After the defeat of the Japanese, when the Dutch tried to reoccupy Bali, they found that a strong movement for independence had been organized. In order to suppress this, they sent the same Captain Raymond Westerling who became infamous in Makassar, where he was also sent to put down an anti-Dutch revolt. The number of Balinese who were killed in the expedition led by Westerling is not known, but the people of Bali claim that more than two thousand lost their lives, many having been machine-gunned to death.

The changes in Indonesian society since the Republic was proclaimed have affected the Balinese, who have made a strenuous effort to rid themselves of the feudal aristocratic landlords; to start small industries and to expand educational facilities. But the dance; the music; the painting; the sculpture and the beautiful women are as touched with magic as when Covarrubias lived on the island.

Chapter Sixteen

IT SEEMED like an ordinary day, although we were sad because our Bali vacation was coming to an end, and early the next morning we had to start on the long journey home. As there was nothing to indicate that difficulties were brewing, we enjoyed a swim and a leisurely breakfast, and afterwards took a walk along the beach, admiring the women who were digging up coral. At about four in the afternoon, we decided to drive into Denpasar and pay our bill.

Going to the office of the manager, my husband asked if he could settle his account. The clerk gave him a quizzical look but said nothing, and in a few moments presented him with a statement. Having checked it, my husband then handed the clerk three thousand rupiahs, all in one thousand rupiah notes. Seeing these, the clerk began laughing, and continued to laugh until tears began to pour down his cheeks. Finally controlling his laughter the clerk asked: "Where have you been all day?"

"On the beach at Sanur."

"And you haven't heard the news?"

"What news?" my husband asked, becoming somewhat concerned. "Your three thousand rupiahs," the clerk said, waving the notes in the air, "are worth exactly three hundred." And with this, he burst into laughter again, and then thrust an official looking document in front of us, which read:

A Government regulation to replace law No. 2 of the year, signed by the President of the Republic of Indonesia, is called the "government regulation for replacing the law on the reduction of the value of banknotes of the Rupiah 500 and Rupiah 1000 denominations".

Article I of the regulation stipulates that the value of banknotes of the Rp. 500 and Rp. 1000 denominations which are now in circulation has been respectively reduced to 50 and 100 Rupiahs.

This regulation is effective as of 06.000 hours Java time on August 25, 1959.

We were stunned, "What shall I do?" my husband asked the clerk. "I haven't another rupiah with me."

Before the clerk had an opportunity to reply, the manager of the hotel appeared and said: "Don't give it a second thought, everyone else in the hotel has enjoyed a lovely vacation at our expense, so there is no reason for you to be disturbed. When you return to Surabaja, you can send a money order. But it really doesn't matter."

And then taking the rupiahs that my husband had put on the desk, he added: "You had better take these with you, not that they will do you much good."

When the tourists standing in the lobby spied the manager they quickly gathered around him like angry bumble-bees. As ill-luck would have it, a large party of schoolteachers from Australia had come to Denpasar the day before and changed their money at the legal rate, a transaction which involved a loss for them. And now, the rupiahs they had been given were worth practically nothing. The teachers could ill afford such a loss and were complaining bitterly to the manager, but there was nothing he could do to help them.

When we returned to Sanur, we found Soegeng waiting for us. He was not a bit upset but merely muttered: "Well, this morning I had two thousand rupiahs and now I have two hundred; if I had spent that money on one of my darlings, I would have been much better off."

However, our hotel bearer was enraged. He told us that the Balinese were furious because some of the army officers stationed on the island had taken unfair advantage of the people. Having learned early in the morning about the depreciation of the money, they went from shop to shop buying gold and silver jewellery, and paid for their purchases with thousand rupiah notes. The shopkeepers, who in Bali, are almost all women, were surprised at the sharp increase in business, but they never suspected that they were being victimized. When they learned about the Government regulation, it was too late. Their losses were enormous. Even women selling fruit and vegetables in the bazaar had been fleeced in the same way.

The bearer declared: "Not only has our faith in the Djakarta Government been shaken, but our respect for the army officers stationed here has vanished. We think it is contemptible that they, of all people, should have abused us."

The tourists were in no mood to be entertained, and so the dance performance which had been scheduled for that night was cancelled. We spent the evening packing and talking with Soegeng. We promised to try and arrange an exhibition of his paintings in Surabaja, for we

Balinese cremation ceremony. Women carrying bones, wrapped in white tissue paper, to be blessed by the Brahman priest.

The wooden cows, inside which the bones have been placed, burning at the auspicious hour

The Barong discussing some of his problems with the monkey

were sure that once his work was seen by a wider audience, his talent as a painter would no longer be overlooked.

Early the next morning, before the dawn appeared, we started on our way, retracing our steps along the bumpy road. When we arrived at Gilimanuk, we had to wait about an hour as the landing ship was being unloaded. Workers carried heavy sacks of rice from the boat to the warehouse. When they were finished, we boarded the ferry, and soon afterwards, snorting and wheezing like an elderly asthmatic, it left the harbour.

It was a cloudless day and we could see the Java coast clearly outlined as we pulled away from the shore. The Balinese sailor, whom we had noticed before, because of his unusual appearance, greeted us like old friends. He was holding a slender piece of tamarind wood in one hand and a small, sharp knife in the other. We had not left the shore for more than ten minutes when the waves began to increase in size. They became higher and higher. We were surrounded by an angry sea. We might have been in the middle of the Atlantic Ocean. We could see neither the Bali shore nor the island of Java; all we could see were waves.

The helmsman, who was only a teen-aged boy, turned the wheel full circle each time a wave approached and they began to come faster and faster. The waves were hitting us broadside, so the tiny ferry could hardly sustain the cruel punishment. It rose and sank like a toy. Sometimes we dropped as much as forty feet. By that time the waves were sweeping over the lower deck where the cars were parked.

Fear gripped me like an ugly, grey cat. I was sure we would never make it to shore. The other passengers looked green. Only my husband and the Balinese sailor were as self-possessed as ever. Occasionally, the sailor shouted a word of advice to the helmsman; otherwise he sat quietly whittling at the stick of wood I had seen in his hand when we came aboard. After one particularly large wave sent us keeling to the side, he came over to me and said: "Don't be afraid, we will soon reach land."

But the waves became higher and rougher, and everyone was panicky. I remembered that someone in Denpasar had told us that the Bali Straits were infested with sharks. I found myself hoping that the sharks, like so many of my Indian friends, would prove to be vegetarians. After what seemed like hours, though in reality, it could not have been more than two, we reached the Java shore. When we were about to disembark, the sailor came over to me and said: "I have made something for you. Whenever you travel across a body of water, keep it with you, and you will always reach your destination safely." And he gave me an exquisite carving of the Hindu goddess Indra rising from the sea, which he had made during that terrible crossing.

When we landed, I said to my husband: "You know, I am still shaking."

"Then you are in exactly the same position as the Indonesian economy," he replied. "Do you realize that because of the cut in money, we have to drive straight through to Surabaja. I don't have enough to pay for a hotel."

And so we went on, arriving in Surabaja at about three in the morning, completely exhausted. But Siti would not let us sleep. She insisted on telling us in detail some of the events that had followed the announcement of the devaluation of the 500 and 1,000 rupiah notes. In typical Indonesian fashion, she stressed the humour rather than the hardships of the situation.

Living near us was an Indonesian family who had always seemed quite poor, but when news of the devaluation was announced, the husband disclosed that he had hoarded close to one hundred thousand rupiahs in thousand rupiah notes. Whereupon his two wives became so angry that they both left him.

Another man, upon hearing the announcement on the radio, dashed into the office of the Garuda Airways and purchased twenty air tickets to Djakarta, paying for them with thousand rupiah notes. The next day he returned and said to the clerk:

"I am so sorry, but I am unable to use those tickets to Djakarta. Will you be so kind as to refund my money?"

After listening to various tales of woe, we eventually persuaded Siti to let us sleep. The following day we learned that this economic regulation was even more stringent than we had realized. In addition to the devaluation of the notes, the decree also provided that the management of banks, State as well as private, were obliged to freeze ninety per cent of deposits in excess of 25,000 rupiahs. Moreover, a heavy tax was levied on imports. These restrictions brought business to a standstill. Many employers did not have adequate cash to pay wages.

In order to have issued such economic decrees, the President had to have specific constitutional authority. Such power had been granted him by the 1945 Constitution. But the 1945 Constitution was no longer in effect having been superseded by the Tentative Constitution of 1952. To meet this obstacle, the President issued the call for a return to the

1945 Constitution, a bold step which was far more complex and significant than it appeared to be on the surface.

The year 1945 had been one of triumph. The Japanese were defeated. The Constitution was drafted. The new Republic came into being. Those who took part in the revolutionary activities, such as the poet Chairil Anwar, were dubbed the "generation of 1945". From 1945 until 1948 the high level of national endeavour was maintained. As in many other Asian countries, the struggle against colonialism brought different groups of the population together in a common cause. Farmers, workers, intellectuals and business men were united; each had a grievance against some aspect of the colonial policy. National aspirations were so pressing that fundamental animosities were temporarily shelved.

In 1948, rifts in the national unity began appearing, the most serious being the affair at Madiun which brought right and left forces into conflict. After this, differences between various sections of the population could no longer be concealed. The cultivators wanted land reform. The city workers wanted better conditions and nationalization of industry. Financiers, industrialists and business men desired a continuation of the economic pattern founded by the Dutch, but with indigenous Indonesian capital in the driver's seat. These conflicting economic demands found expression in the development of political parties, which in turn led to recurrent crises.

For a long time the President had been seeking a way to halt these political upheavals. He had come to the conclusion that reform was not possible under the western form of parliamentary government. When we first came to Djakarta and heard Sukarno speak on the occasion of the twelfth anniversary of independence, he had castigated "liberal democracy" and proposed "guided democracy". Some time later, speaking to the Pantjasila Seminar in Jogjakarta on February 20th, 1959, the President declared: "I consider guided democracy as absolutely necessary for the realization of a just and prosperous society."

The President wanted to eliminate political instability by transferring power to a Cabinet composed of delegates from the chief parliamentary parties and by the organization of a National Council, representing functional groups. This Council was to be given consultative status. But because of the rebellion which had started early in 1958 and the proclamation of martial law, all changes were postponed and the policy, as proposed by the President, was not carried out.

In 1959, the idea of guided democracy came to the fore again, but at this stage Sukarno decided it could only be achieved if there were a return to the 1945 Constitution, which accorded him extremely broad powers. Under its provisions he was the Head of State, Commander-in-Chief of the Defence Forces, and could also serve as the Prime Minister. The Government was not responsible to the Parliament but to the President. Furthermore, at "critical times" he was given the right, under Article 22, to "enact Government provisions replacing the law."

In his decision to return to the 1945 Constitution, the President had the support of his own Party, the Partai Nasional Indonesia; the Nahdatul Ulama Party, representing the conservative Muslims, and the Partai Komunis Indonesia, whose strength was concentrated in East Java, but whose following was not limited to that area. He was bitterly opposed by the Indonesian Socialist Party, a small right wing remnant of the Socialist Party without any mass following, and by the Masjumi Party. (This opposition foreshadowed the demise of both of these parties, for on August 17th, 1960, speaking at the celebration of the fifteenth anniversary of independence, the President gave the Masjumi and the Indonesian Socialist party thirty days in which "to dissolve themselves". He declared: "The Government takes measures against those parties which endanger the State.")

There was one force which kept its own counsel, and that was the military. Because of the West Irian campaign and the Sumatran rebellion, the military had become more powerful. Slowly it began to encroach on civilian prerogatives, and we witnessed the phenomenon of military leaders usurping duties that formerly belonged to civilians.

The military censored newspapers, banning their appearance for weeks or even months because they had printed articles which the military felt were harmful to the national effort. In East Java, when a new Governor was appointed, the military did not permit him to take office for months. When a newspaper commented on this strange situation, the editor was warned that no speculation as to the future career of the Governor-designate would be allowed.

The military arrested civilians in high Government posts. Thus, the Attorney-General of Indonesia, who had a reputation for honesty and efficiency was arrested by the military, presumably because he was investigating irregularities in army contracts. One afternoon, the popular head of Customs for East Java was arrested by the Navy. It was rumoured that there had been dissension within the armed forces over control of the Surabaja port.

The military also dabbled in politics. Defence Minister, General Abdul Harris Nasution, created his own party. But on the issue of guided democracy, the military leadership said nothing; it was biding its time. The President, however, knowing he had support of the lower ranks of all the services, went ahead. Although it is sometimes said that the President is a prisoner of the military, time and again he has shown that he was capable of following an independent course of action whether or not it pleases the military.

Finally, on the evening of July 5th, 1959, President Sukarno issued a decree declaring the re-application of the 1945 Constitution for the whole of Indonesia. At the same time he announced the dissolution of the Constituent Assembly, the formation of the Provisional People's Consultative Congress, and the formation of the Provisional Supreme Advisory Council. The political battle to return to the 1945 Constitution had been won; the economic battle was yet undecided.

The President hoped that by increasing the scope of the public sector of the economy that the situation could be improved. Article 33 of the 1945 Constitution provided him ample scope for nationalization because it states that, "Branches of production which are important to the State and which dominate the life of most people, are regulated by the State," and that, "Land and water and natural riches therein are regulated by the State and shall be used for the greatest possible prosperity of the people."

The first regulation issued after the return to the 1945 Constitution was the devaluation of currency and freezing of bank accounts which took place while we were in Bali. For a short time afterwards there was an improvement. Prices fell as merchants put on their shelves goods they had been hoarding. The rupiah seemed more stable. But gradually the value of the rupiah began to fall again and towards the end of 1959 one could easily get 400 rupiahs for an American dollar on the black market, though officially it was pegged at twenty-five to the dollar.

On Government exchange rates a tin of imported cheese cost ten dollars; "Nescafé", almost twelve; a bottle of good whisky, twenty, and a table fan, three hundred. Of course, the average Indonesians were not interested in buying imported cheese or coffee, nor were they in the market for electric fans, but they did need cloth and the price of textiles had risen in the same proportion as other imported items.

When my husband had a suit made, he paid 6,000 rupiahs, which on

Government exchange was equivalent to two hundred dollars. The poorest kind of cloth was selling for sixty and eighty rupiahs a metre, and an ordinary batik, which cost, when we first came to Surabaja, two hundred rupiahs had quadrupled in price. The only commodity which did not go up in price were "Bata" shoes, so when a consignment came into the shop it was sold out in the first hour and until the next one arrived, the only shoes remaining were those in the window. Fortunately, the co-operatives were able to sell some cloth at a reasonable price. Were it not for this, the clothing situation would have become disastrous for the working people.

Due to prompt and efficient action by the Government, the price of rice had increased only fifty per cent. A kilo of rice was selling for six to eight rupiahs in the bazaar but could be bought for four and a half rupiahs in the co-operatives. But even at this price, manual labourers found it difficult to get along because they only earned ten rupiahs a day. Because of this, workers were drawn to those factories which provided a rice ration in addition to wages. To keep the price of rice from rising even more, the Government had to import thousands of tons, which in turn meant that sorely needed foreign currency was being spent for rice.

The middle class, particularly teachers, government workers, clerks, shop assistants and others on fixed salaries, were in dire distress. Many of them had to borrow money because their salary was gone by the middle of the month. As prices continued to rise, housewives, against the wishes of the military, paraded in the streets of Surabaja and Djakarta, protesting against the high cost of food and clothing.

The return to the 1945 Constitution had not provided a panacea nor had the monetary reforms been of lasting value, because basic economic aggravations continued to exist. The Government still had to depend for its foreign exchange on the export of a relatively few products—rubber, petroleum and tin. Industrial development was slow because of lack of progress in the fields of transportation, communications and power, the basic factors necessary for industrialization. The *per capita* income of the people was low and therefore their purchasing power very limited. But the fundamental economic instability was related to agriculture in which seventy per cent of the people are involved. Their tools, production techniques, and farm units may have been adequate for a subsistence economy but are far from adequate for a modern economy.

It was just at the end of 1959 and the beginning of the New Year that a new regulation was to go into effect. Earlier, in July, 1959, a decree had been passed by the Government restricting alien traders in rural areas from doing business. The ostensible purpose of the decree was to pave the way for co-operatives to take over rural trade. But the actual effect was to alter the position of the two and a half million Chinese living throughout Indonesia.

Chapter Seventeen

WE WERE SPENDING a few days in Selecta, a mountain resort in East Java, with a swimming pool surrounded by hills on which beautiful gardens had been laid out. Walking along the ridge of one of these hills we noticed a plane circling overhead. A physician, who was with us, watched it closely, sighed and said:

"If I were given the finest city in Java, the loveliest girl in Bali, and the most productive oil well in Sumatra, I could not be induced to fly a plane again."

"You know how to pilot a plane?"

"Yes," he answered. "I became a pilot just before the last war. At that time I was studying medicine. One day I noticed a signboard on which a large advertisement had been pasted: LEARN TO FLY WITHOUT COST. And underneath in smaller letters, the poster explained that flying lessons would be given free to young men willing to join the Royal Dutch Air Force.

"So I enlisted and while continuing my studies, learned how to fly. Then in 1942 the Japanese invaded the islands. We, who were pilots, were flown out of Java, and imagine my surprise when we were taken to the United States for further training. I was sent to Texas. When my training was completed, I was flown back to a base in South-East Asia and from then on I piloted a bomber. I was so proud to be fighting with the Allies.

"After what seemed like an eternity, the Japanese were defeated and peace was declared. How wonderful it was to be able to return to Java. But when I arrived here, I found that a bitter armed conflict had broken out because the Dutch wished to reassert their control over the country.

"I asked for an immediate release from the Air Force. This was categorically denied. I was informed that in my contract, I had agreed to stay in the armed services as long as a state of war existed. According to the Dutch military authorities, the war was not over, and under the terms of my contract, I had to continue flying. This meant, in effect, that I would have to bomb my own people. I was told that refusal to comply with orders would be considered a breach of contract, and would be punished by imprisonment. I went to prison.

"On December 19th, 1948, the second full-scale military offensive was launched by the Dutch. Bombers attacked Jogjakarta early in the morning. In other parts of the country paratroopers occupied key points. Among those captured was President Sukarno who was taken to Sumatra. This armed offensive was in direct violation of the Renville Truce which had been negotiated under the auspices of the United Nations on February 28th, 1948, and which had been approved by the Security Council.

"Called to account by the United Nations, the Dutch Government took the position that this was not a military offensive but merely a 'police action'. On the basis of this statement, my attorney then argued that I was not bound by the contract. The Dutch could not have it both ways. They could not base their United Nation's case on the premise that there was no war in Indonesia, but only a 'police action', and at the same time enforce my contract which stipulated that I must serve as long as there was a state of war."

"What finally happened?"

"We won the case and I was released from prison; then I fought with an Indonesian unit."

"You must have been a hero!"

"No," he replied, shaking his head. "It is not possible for someone who is of Chinese origin to be considered a hero here in Indonesia."

We knew many Chinese in Surabaja. Most foreigners living in Indonesia had friends among the Chinese, because they are very sociable, and not shy about meeting strangers. I always divided those we knew into three distinct groups; the Dutch-Chinese, the Chinese-Chinese and the Indonesian-Chinese.

The Dutch-Chinese belonged to the middle class. They were clerks, sales people, lawyers and engineers. Dutch was their mother tongue and they clung to Dutch customs. Their ideas and ideals had been moulded by the Dutch, and their approach to life was Calvinistic, for they were hard-working, well disciplined and frugal. They were almost all Christians. They were absolutely disinterested in politics. Tenaciously they refused to be drawn into political debates or political parties, remaining completely aloof.

Typical of this group was our Indonesian teacher, who was born in Ambon but had lived most of his life in East Java. When we met him, he was teaching Bahasa Indonesia in a high school. He spoke Dutch,

Javanese and Indonesian, but not a word of Chinese. Conscientious to a fault, he was a serious and sincere teacher.

Once he invited us to his home for dinner. We went, expecting a typical Chinese repast, but instead the dinner consisted of thick soup, potatoes, boiled meat, string beans cooked with a bit of pork, and a pudding. His home was furnished in European style with an upright piano and two reproductions, one by Brueghel and the other by Rubens

His wife, a slender and pretty woman, spoke Dutch and was learning English. Her Indonesian was not much better than mine. They had two children, a boy and a girl, who were studying at one of the city schools, so they were proficient in Bahasa. After dinner, his daughter played the piano for us. She played "Für Elise" by Beethoven, which brought back vividly my own childhood days when I had learned this same piece.

Our teacher had lived through one of the most tumultuous periods of Indonesian history, and had remained unscarred. He had moved from one crisis to another, like a figure on a screen, shielded from reality. He had been a teacher during the Dutch rule, and had continued to teach during the Japanese occupation. He had been in Surabaja when it was shelled by British warships, and when Dutch and Indonesian troops were fighting in the streets. He was there when independence was declared. Now, he was still teaching, and although he was disturbed by the increasing manifestations of anti-Chinese feeling, he was sure that this too would not affect him, and his life would continue as before.

The Chinese-Chinese were entirely different. Those we knew were from the wealthy upper class. They were industrialists, financiers, importers and in some instances doctors. One of our good friends belonged to this group. His family had been bankers for generations. His home was filled with antique Chinese furniture and precious porcelains. Being a patron of the arts, he had bought several of Affandi's earliest paintings. His wife was tall, slim and fastidiously dressed in a tight-fitting "chaksan" with a high collar, and a tight skirt that was slit on each side. When we dined, it was on delicious Chinese food, including Peking duck.

Our host had been abroad many times. He had studied at one of the Dutch Universities and at Harvard. But he remained essentially Chinese. Within the family he spoke Chinese and by religion he was a Buddhist.

We talked at length about the position of the Chinese in Indonesia. He said: "There are some people who think that the Dutch bestowed favours upon us, but that is not true. We wrested concessions from them because we were a cohesive group. We were especially successful in obtaining education for our children. After the victory of the Japanese against the Russians in 1905, the Dutch no longer considered the Japanese 'inferior to white people', and gave them equal status. We fought for similar privileges, especially with regard to education. In 1912 we succeeded in forcing the Government to open 'Dutch-Chinese' schools. The medium of instruction was Dutch, the students Chinese.

"Over the years we consolidated our economic position, especially in small industries and banking. Then came the Japanese occupation. Although we hated the Japanese, we followed a policy of discretion which was interpreted by some Indonesians as collaboration. After the Japanese defeat we did not oppose the return of the Dutch because our financial interests would have suffered.

"Our situation became critical during the Sumatran rebellion. As you know, arms sent to the rebels came in boxes marked Taiwan. When this was discovered, the Government banned all Chinese newspapers edited or published by those who were identified with Chiang Kai-shek. Schools owned and operated by this group were also closed. These wealthy Chinese who had given support to Chiang became desperate. They sold their Indonesian rupiahs for foreign currency at any rate they could get. On the black market the exchange was five hundred rupiahs for an American dollar. Many fled to Holland or the United States. They did not go to Taiwan because they felt the future there would be bleak.

"Those, like myself, who are against socialism but admire the new China have remained here. But my guess is that as it becomes more difficult for us to do business, we will also have to move. But where can we go?"

Far below the Chinese-Chinese and the Dutch-Chinese were those whom I classified as Indonesian-Chinese, most of them being ordinary working people. Their language was Indonesian, or the mother tongue of the island where they had been brought up. In Sumatra they worked in the oil fields or on the rubber and tobacco plantations. In Kalimantan they were oil workers or diamond miners. In Ambon they were engaged in the production of pepper, while on the small islands of Bangka and Biliton they mined tin.

Having lived in Indonesia for generations, many had intermarried and become Muslims, although some remained Confucians and some became Christians. Economically, the majority of this group were no better off than the rest of the population. But among the Indonesian-Chinese were the rural traders, who bought and sold produce and often lent money to the cultivators. They were wealthier than the Indonesian villagers, but not really rich. They were petty business men who had lived in the villages long enough to become a part of the local scene.

Long before the Dutch came to Indonesia, Chinese had settled in various parts of the country. But it was not until the establishment of the Dutch East India Company that the Chinese migrated to the Archipelago in great numbers. They were encouraged to do so by Governor-General Jan Pietersz. Coen, who used them as a buffer between the Company and the Javanese. The Chinese were employed as middle-men. They were not only diligent but also wizards at mathematics. Moreover, they were skilled in the production of sugar and spices. The Governor-General declared: "There is no people in the world which serves us better than the Chinese: too many of them cannot be brought to Batavia." He was so enthusiastic that he suggested kidnapping Chinese from the mainland if they refused to come voluntarily. The Chinese soon constituted the most important minority group in Batavia. They became the principle middle men between the Dutch and the Indonesians.

Coen had never hidden his contempt for the Javanese:

"May not a man in Europe do what he likes with his cattle? Even so does the master here do with his men, for everywhere, these with all that belongs to them are as much the property of the master, as are the brute beasts in the Netherlands. The law of this land is the will of the king and he is king who is the strongest."

This arrogant attitude did not go unnoticed, particularly by the Indonesian rajas, who realized that their position was threatened by the increasing power of the Dutch East India Company. The bravest of the local rulers, the Sultan Agung of Mataram decided to challenge the Dutch. Before attacking the fortress at Batavia, the Commander-in-Chief of the Mataramese army of Sultan Agung, addressed a letter to the "Captain of the Chinese at Batavia", in which he appealed to the Chinese community to side with the Javanese against the foreign interlopers. He wrote:

"We have not come because of the Chinese; the Chinese we shall not trouble; we have come to vanquish and conquer the Dutch or Hollanders. I advise you that you do not leave Djakarta, for all the storehouses which remain undamaged shall belong to you and to the Chinese who stay with you——"

Confident of victory, he warned the Chinese that the fortress would be taken: "Do not imagine," the Commander-in-Chief wrote in his letter, "that they will hold their own, for soon conditions shall be such that their mighty castle will fall, wait but four or five days, and then the arms, the greatest nobles, and the most important warriors of Mataram will come. There are so many we cannot give their names; but they will be three hundred thousand strong."

And tens of thousands came, armed with primitive weapons and ancestral swords, but the Sultan of Agung and his valiant army was defeated, for the Sultan was unable to bring enough supplies by land, and his ships were sunk by the Dutch.

The Chinese in Batavia had turned a deaf ear to the plea of the Sultan and remained loyal to the Dutch. More than a hundred years later this was to be repaid in bitter coin. But during the ensuing period they prospered. Many of them started sugar plantations and mills, exporting the produce to other countries. By the middle of the eighteenth century there were 80,000 Chinese in Java.

The Dutch looked upon these Chinese immigrants with suspicion. They spoke a strange language and had mysterious ways. They were, according to the white settlers, cunning and devious and only waiting for a chance to capture Batavia and usurp Dutch power. In 1740, rumours began circulating that the Chinese were planning to revolt. At the same time there were other rumours that the Chinese were going to be deported to Ceylon and that on the way they would be thrown overboard. The Chinese became frightened and began forming armed groups. When the Dutch settlers within the fortress heard this, they attacked the Chinese, and massacred them. When it was over, of the nine thousand Chinese living in Batavia only one hundred and fifty were spared.

Despite this massacre, the Chinese migration continued. Thirty years later Captain Cook remarked that it was hard to find in Batavia a Chinese who was idle, and a Dutchman or Indonesian who was working. This predilection for hard work was a trait the Chinese acquired from having been brought up in a country that demanded diligence as the price of survival.

In Java, there was an expendable supply of labour, so the Dutch only needed the Chinese as middlemen. They were given the right to levy taxes and to lease large tracts of land. The Chinese, acting as intermediaries for the Dutch, collected poll-taxes, slaughter-house taxes, river taxes and bazaar taxes. At the same time they became the largest single group of traders in the rural areas. Some of the Chinese settlers in Java obtained great wealth. Governor-General Daendels, when in need of money for administrative purposes, sold the whole agency of Probolinggo in East Java to a Chinese, Man Ti Ko, for the sum of one million dollars.

But the Chinese were only "the agents of the Dutch". Even though individual Chinese prospered, they were only enjoying the crumbs from a table laden with food. The real wealth belonged to the Dutch. it was the Dutch who owned the plantations, the factories, the sugar mills and the banks. The Chinese were not allowed to own land; they could lease the land, but they could not buy or sell it. Moreover, they were subject to a number of humiliations. They were not allowed to travel without permission of the Dutch, nor could they reside in certain parts of Java without Government approval. These restrictions were not abolished until 1911. Neither did they enjoy equal status with the Europeans before the law or in the jails.

On the other islands, the situation was quite different. Rich in natural resources, most of them were sparsely populated. In Sumatra the Dutch found it almost impossible to draft local labour. The Sumatrans, whose standard of living was higher than that of the Javanese, refused to work on the plantations, and when compelled to do so, collapsed, unable to withstand the arduous labour. And so the Dutch imported Chinese, whose number rose from 70,000 in 1860 to 260,000 in 1900, and by 1920 they constituted the main labour force on the plantations and in the mines.

The Chinese were often brought to the islands under false pretences. Promised good working conditions and the right to return home after a certain number of years, they soon discovered that the contracts which they had signed actually doomed them to a life-time of slavery. Most of the Chinese came from Fukien province. The port from which they sailed was Amoy, and a number of modern Chinese writers have described the sufferings and hardships of these migrant Chinese.

With the establishment of the Republic of China in 1911, an agreement was reached between the Dutch Government and the Chinese

Government under which China gave up her claims upon the Indonesian-born Chinese and agreed to recognize them as Dutch subjects, while the Netherlands Government admitted Chinese consuls to take care of the numerous Chinese-born immigrants who remained Chinese citizens.

The question of the nationality of the Chinese living in Indonesia was to become more and more complicated. After Indonesian independence, the Government allowed those Chinese, who were still officially Chinese citizens, to acquire Indonesian citizenship through a passive system. A period of one year was granted, during which time the Chinese who did not wish to become Indonesian citizens were allowed to submit a statement to the Government. Later the Government decided that every Chinese, who on August 17th, 1948, had not rejected Indonesian citizenship, automatically became a citizen. Many Chinese became Indonesian citizens under this formula, while at the same time remaining citizens of China, thus acquiring dual citizenship.

In 1955, an agreement was concluded between the Indonesian Government and the People's Republic of China obliging all adults with dual citizenship to choose either Indonesian or Chinese nationality within two years' time. Those who wished to remain Indonesian citizens had to reject Chinese citizenship before an Indonesian official.

On January 20th, 1960, the Chinese Government and the Indonesian Government ratified the 1955 Treaty on the question of dual nationality, which in effect provided that those Chinese who wished to do so could opt for Indonesian citizenship; those who did not, could remain Chinese nationals; and all children born of Chinese parents could on reaching the age of eighteen decide which nationality to choose.

But even this clarification did not alter the situation, because the movement against retail traders in the rural areas, unleashed anti-Chinese feelings that were directed against all Chinese regardless of whether they were or were not citizens.

The antagonism against the Chinese was particularly strong among the middle class and noticeably absent among the working people. The PKI was critical of this anti-Chinese movement, pointing out the scapeboat nature of the undertaking. But our professional friends felt differently. One of them said to me: "You have no idea how the Chinese exploited us over the years. We hate them. We would rather have white people like you in Indonesia, than the Chinese."

Another exclaimed: "The Chinese have always had the best of everything. They have lived off the fat of our land. Now, we intend to be masters in our own house and if they don't like it, they can leave."

While he was talking I was reminded of the many Burmese I knew, who spoke in exactly the same way about the Indians, and there is an historic parallel between the position of the Chinese in Indonesia and the Indians living in Burma. In ancient Burma, land could not be bought or sold. But after the British conquered the country, they introduced private ownership of the land and taxation based on cash payment. They brought in Indians to collect the taxes. The Burmese cultivator was forced to borrow money to pay his taxes and most of the money-lenders were Indians. By the beginning of the Second World War, half the cultivated land in lower Burma was in the hands of non-agriculturists, the majority of whom were Indians, Chettiyars from Madras.

Furthermore, because the Burmese, like the Sumatrans, did not find it difficult to earn a living, they refused to take those jobs requiring hard physical labour, so many Indians were brought from Malabar to Burma as street sweepers, dock workers and unskilled labourers. The Burmese looked down upon them and after the Burmese achieved independence their anti-Indian feelings were directed against the poor as well as the rich Indians.

Mass migrations have taken place in Asia for two reasons; because poverty drove people to look elsewhere for a living, and because the exigencies of colonial powers demanded cheap and reliable labour which they achieved by moving one group of people to another country. Thus, the Indians spread to Ceylon, Malaya, Burma, the Fiji Islands and Africa; while the Chinese went to Malaya, Burma, French Indo-China, Indonesia and the Philippines.

Not long after the new year began, I was in the shop where we had purchased our furniture. I asked the proprietor if he would send someone to repair our dining-room table. He said that he would like to help me but that he no longer had any carpenters working for him.

"Where have they gone?" I asked.

"As yet, they have not gone anywhere. They are waiting for ships from the People's Republic of China to take them there."

"Are they all Chinese citizens?"

"No, but they are all convinced that there is no future for their children in Indonesia."

Performance of the famous Ketjak dance of Bali

Two Balinese children who take the main dancing rôles in the Barong drama

President Sukarno relaxing with friends

Dr. Soendoro nails his name to the mace after being promoted. Holding the mace is the Adjutant of the University

A few days later the owner of a shoe shop told me the same story. All of his leather workers had left and he was also planning to close his store and return to China.

"But you are wealthy. Doesn't this mean that you have to give up all the money you have earned during your life-time?"

Yes, he agreed it meant just that, but he had been convinced a few years before that the situation was becoming intolerable for Chinese business men. At that time, there had been a meeting of representatives of Indonesian business firms in Surabaja. At the meeting, which was called the All-Indonesian Importers Congress, a decision had been taken not to make a distinction between the capital of those Chinese who had adopted Indonesian citizenship and those who had remained Chinese nationals.

"So the real problem," he concluded, "is not that of citizenship, but of the desire to eliminate Chinese economic competition. There is an old Chinese fable about a man who wanted some gold. One morning, arriving at the gold-dealer's stall, he seized a piece of gold and started to run away. The officer who caught him asked: 'Why did you steal the gold in front of so many people?' To which the thief replied: 'When I took the gold, I saw nobody. All I saw was the gold.' "

Chinese from all classes were leaving. Wealthy Chinese were giving away their factories. Sons and daughters of these rich industrialists were learning trades. Special night schools had been open for the purpose of teaching different crafts. Men and women, who had never known anything but a life of luxury, seemed perfectly willing to part with their material possessions without a whimper. And this they had to do as they were not allowed to take cameras, jewels, books or money with them. Even the number of clothes they were permitted to take was limited.

Students and technicians were also planning to leave and some doctors of Chinese origin also applied for permission to go. But we were most surprised when we learned that the Professor of Chemistry at the Fakultas Kedokteran was leaving. We could not believe that he would be willing to say farewell to a country in which he was born and which he loved. When we spoke with him, he said:

"I am doing this for my sons, not for myself. I am sure that if I wished to stay there would be no difficulties. I have life tenure as a professor. But what about my sons? What will happen to them? There is already a quota for Chinese students at the medical college and as a result of this campaign it will be made even smaller. I was in

Holland during the Nazi occupation and I know what racial discrimination means. I don't want my sons to feel that they will be denied equal rights because they are of Chinese ancestry."

Among those Chinese living in Indonesia who decided to leave were carpenters; leather workers; sugar workers; miners; farmers; students; technicians; teachers and doctors, and among them many could not speak a word of Chinese. From the point of view of China, this was like receiving an unexpected gift. The majority of the tens of thousands who were returning were in the prime of life, educated, skilled and ready to work. Indonesia suffered a corresponding loss. She could ill afford to lose so many trained people. In the rural areas there was acute dislocation because the co-operatives were not ready to replace the private traders.

During this period relations between the Indonesian Government and the People's Republic of China remained on an even keel. This enabled agreements to be reached and helped to minimize the hardships suffered by those who had to migrate. Discussing this situation with one of my friends, he said that nationalism creates its own pitfalls, but when sober judgement prevails those pitfalls—such as national chauvinism—are bound to disappear.

Chapter Eighteen

Puasa, which always falls on the ninth Arabic month of Ramadan, when Allah revealed the sacred Koran to the Prophet Mohammed, was being observed. Very much like Lent, it is a time of meditation and abstinence. Orthodox followers of Islam do not eat, drink or smoke from sunrise until sunset.

Every evening in Surabaja, just at sunset, we could hear the boom of a cannon announcing the official closing of the day, so that all those who had been fasting were permitted to eat. For those who observed Puasa, night was turned into day. Families awoke around midnight and again before dawn in order to eat enough to keep themselves going until the following evening. At two or three in the morning, one could see lights in many houses where the inhabitants were either preparing food or praying.

But unlike Lent, abstinence during Puasa is confined to the daylight hours. Once the sun has closed its eyes, revelry may begin, lasting throughout the night. In the kampung across from us hardly anyone bothered to pray or to fast, but everyone enjoyed the nocturnal pleasures of Puasa. There was singing, dancing, gambling and performances of the Wayang Orang.

Because it was Puasa, we decided to drive to Gresik, a town near Surabaja, and visit the graves of Sunan Giri and Ibrahim Malik, who were the first of the nine "walis" or holy men, to expound the doctrines of Islam in Indonesia. We asked one of our friends, a noted historian, to accompany us. On the way, he told us that Ibrahim Malik had come from Gujarat, India, to Java during the fifteenth century and had settled in Gresik which was then a thriving sea-port. Sunan Giri, whose real name was Raden Paku, was born in East Java, belonging to a rich and aristocratic family. It was only after studying the Koran that he took the name of Sunan Giri, Prince of the Mountain, and he established a school for Muslim scholars on the highest hill in Gresik. There, scholars from all over the islands, used to come to study Islamic texts. Today, at this very site, there is still a school for Muslim scholars, situated next to the tomb of Sunan Giri.

As we were climbing the many steps leading to his burial place a little girl asked my husband to buy some flowers to place on the

179

tomb. After doing so, he turned to our friend and asked: "Would you like to carry some of these?" Our friend shook his head and answered: "No, indeed, if I carry those flowers I may be taken for a pilgrim, an orthodox Muslim. And that is not so, for I am a freethinker."

After we had visited the mausoleum in which Sunan Giri is buried and which is guarded by two curious looking animals who conform to the Hindu tradition of sculpture and the Muslim edict of non-representational art, I asked our friend, the historian, what he meant when he said he was a freethinker. He replied that a freethinker is someone who believes in questioning the existence of a divine being and who also is sceptical of accepting everything that appears in the religious tracts. Then he went on to say: "As you probably know, the term 'freethinker' is old-fashioned. I suppose one could say that it belongs to the European philosophy of the eighteenth century. Lord Shaftesbury called the freethinker, 'the noblest of characters'."

"But isn't it surprising that such a concept has taken root here."

"It is not surprising at all," he answered. "If you consider our religious history it becomes quite understandable. First, we were animists, then Buddhists, then Hindus and now Muslims. But all the time our own 'adat' was like yeast in bread. Our ideas, traditions and customs moulded each religion. For example, have you ever seen the Djokodolok in Surabaja?"

I shook my head.

"You must go there," he said smiling. "You will see a large, fat, jolly Hindu idol sitting on a throne. Around his neck there are many strings of beads and near him incense is burning. At the foot of his throne, you will notice many small packages. In each one there is a blouse placed before the god by a happily married woman. When an unmarried girl comes to see the idol, she will take one of the blouses and wear it. Because of the blessing of Djokodolok and the fact that the blouse belongs to someone who is already married, she is sure to find a husband. And when she succeeds, she in turn will leave her blouse for another unmarried girl.

"I cite this story because it is an indication of our attitude towards religion. In what other Islamic country could you find a Hindu idol who is still engaged in good work? Djokodolok has been allowed to live and thrive though Indonesia has been a Muslim country for five hundred years. This being the case, you can understand that the assimilation of religions has led to questioning and this in turn to free thought."

"But wasn't it those Indonesians who went abroad who became the freethinkers?"

"Not always, although those who studied in Holland had access to the works of Voltaire, Darwin and Huxley. But for people like me, who have never been out of the country, the source of inspiration has been the Arab philosophers, Omar Khayyám, al-Khindi and Averroes, all of whom were freethinkers."

"As you are a freethinker, why have you come to visit the tombs of Malik and Sunan Giri?"

"Because they represent part of our rich cultural heritage, and as a historian I am interested in learning as much as I can about our past and those who influenced it."

After Puasa came Lebaran, a time of great rejoicing. The first day of Lebaran is the Muslim New Year. Cards and gifts are exchanged; new clothes are purchased and old quarrels are forgotten. This Lebaran of 1960 was to be our last in Indonesia as our Java tour was coming to an end. It didn't seem possible that three years had passed so quickly.

For my husband, the three years had been very fruitful. When he came to the Fakultas Kedokteran there was no department of pharmacology. Having succeeded in establishing an active department, his enthusiasm had attracted a number of medical students to this field, some of whom were willing to forgo the prospects of a lucrative practice in order to teach.

As soon as the date of our departure was known, invitations began arriving. A farewell party was given for us by the members of the Pharmacology Department. The entire staff had come to the home of Dr. Soendoro, including the technicians and the servants. When we arrived the guests were seated in the living-room. Many wore national dress. A place on the sofa had been left for the professor and a place next to him for me. Although my husband's relations with his staff had always been friendly and he had tried to break down the high barrier that exists between the professor and his students, the party made us realize that such a social change is not accomplished overnight. At first, it was a rather formal affair. When we talked everyone listened. When we didn't talk there was silence. Only our host was more at ease for he had been studying at Yale Medical School on a WHO fellowship, and there he had become accustomed to informal gatherings between professors and graduate students.

The ice melted a little when a gift was presented to us; a finely wrought silver bowl which had been made in Jogjakarta. When we went in for dinner a spirit of gaiety prevailed. On the table there was a large platter with a pyramid of rice decorated by half of a hard-boiled egg placed on each side. We were told to cut off the top of the rice pyramid and eat it first. Then we each had to eat half of the egg, for if we did this we would be assured of happiness and a long life together. We followed the instructions, amidst laughter and the popping of flash bulbs, as a photographer had been invited to take pictures.

Afterwards, when we returned to the living-room the ice congealed again. Just before we left, my husband shook hands with each member of his staff and wished each success. A few had tears in their eyes and all were quite moved by this parting. As we drove away, they continued to wave as long as our car was in sight.

A few evenings later a farewell dinner was given by the Fakultas Kedokteran for five professors. It was a gala affair. The President of the University, the Dean of the medical college, the former Dean, the professors and their wives, were all present. The women were gorgeously dressed. The dinner was held at the Yacht Club, which is located near the harbour, so that drinks were served on the terrace from where we could see the lights of the ships anchored quite far out.

After a sumptuous repast, the Dean, Dr. Zaman, rose to make the farewell speech. First, speaking in Bahasa Indonesia he praised the work and effort of the two Indonesian professors who were retiring. Then, speaking in Dutch, the Dean bid adieu to the Professor of Botany, a warm-hearted Dutch lady, who was born in Java, had gone to school with Sukarno and had taught botany for more than twenty-five years in various Indonesian schools.

The only long period of time she had been away from Java was during the Second World War, when she was caught in Holland by the invading Germany army and put in a concentration camp. The Dutch Government in Java had imprisoned some German women, so in retaliation the Germans picked up exactly the same number of Dutch women in the Netherlands and sent them to a camp. After the war, she returned to Indonesia and had been teaching botany at the Fakultas Kedokteran. She was heart-sick at having to leave, for Java was really her home, but because of the political situation her contract was not renewed and there was no possibility of her returning.

Next, speaking in Indonesian once again, the Dean said good-bye to the Professor of Chemistry who was going to China. The Professor's wife, who was seated beside him, was crying. When the

Professor arose, he spoke movingly of his love for Indonesia and his feeling of respect and friendship for his colleagues at the Fakultas Kedokteran.

Finally, the Dean said "selamat djalan" to the Professor of Pharmacology. This time he spoke in English. He thanked the Professor for having successfully developed a department and for having established such warm and cordial relations with so many Indonesians, not only those working for the medical school. "We never felt you were a foreigner," he said. "We accepted you as one of us."

In the midst of all the excitement of the farewell parties and packing our household goods my husband had to help his counterpart, Dr. Soendoro prepare his thesis, for on the basis of this work Dr. Soendoro would be eligible for a promotion and would become head of the department the following year. Dr. Soendoro chose as his topic the relative value of various drugs in the treatment of typhoid fever. He had been working with typhoid patients in the hospital and had acquired a great deal of information but had not organized it in a form suitable for presentation to the professors of the medical faculty. So he had to work very hard to get these data in order.

Finishing just before the deadline, he presented his thesis to the Board and it was accepted. Then Dr. Soendoro was notified that he would be allowed to defend his thesis at eleven o'clock on June 20th, the very day we were scheduled to leave. If he defended his thesis successfully then his promotion would be granted.

Early in the morning of June 20th, we were awakened by a loud knock at the door. Soegeng was there. He had come all the way from Bali to bid us farewell. We insisted that he come with us to the college and that he wear Balinese dress. My husband was in a tuxedo, worn under his academic gown. At ten-thirty, we left for the college by betjak, as our car had already been taken to the harbour for shipment. On the way the betjak driver said: "Siti told us you are leaving today. All of us in the kampung wish you selamat djalan and hope that you will return to Surabaja."

In front of the Fakultas Kedokteran, the University blue and yellow standard was flying alongside the Indonesian flag. In the main hall there were hundreds of guests, including members of the diplomatic corps. Soegeng and I sat down next to Mrs. Soendoro. Her hands were as cold as ice. She whispered: "I have had six children but I was never so frightened as I am today."

On the stroke of eleven, the University adjutant, wearing a four-cornered black hat and a gown trimmed in velvet, came into the hall and banged his staff on the floor three times so that the golden bells attached to it jangled loudly. At this point, the audience rose and then all the professors, wearing their caps and gowns, and representing every faculty affiliated with the Airlangga University, filed in behind President Pringgodigdo. They walked up to the dais and then sat down.

The President arose, his sombre black gown contrasting vividly with the shining gold collar he was wearing, which symbolized his office. He then announced that we were all assembled for the purpose of hearing Dr. Soendoro defend his thesis.

In a few moments the adjutant entered again, followed by Dr. Soendoro, who was flanked on either side by a member of the Pharmacology Department. These two doctors were his seconds, for just as in a duel, Dr. Soendoro was entitled to have seconds who were permitted to answer any question that he might find too difficult.

Dressed in a dark brown suit and wearing a black pitji, Dr. Soendoro went up to the podium and stood in front of the microphone, his faithful seconds beside him. As my husband was the promoter he was given the privilege of asking the first question. This question was so phrased that it gave Dr. Soendoro an opportunity to outline the main points of his thesis.

When he was finished, several other professors asked him questions. He answered each one slowly and carefully without any trace of nervousness. Then, when there were no more questions, the professors marched out of the hall, leaving Dr. Soendoro to wonder whether or not he would be promoted. All of us waited tensely as the minutes dragged by. It seemed as though the professors would never return but finally they filed in again.

The President handed a parchment to my husband who rose and said: "I accept the honour given me by the President of Airlangga University with great pleasure. According to the right in law given to us, and in agreement with the decision of the Senate, we herewith declare Mr. Soendoro, born in Probolinggo in the year of 1922, to be Doctor of Medicine and we also bestow on him all rights and privileges in accordance with law, custom and usage. In witness, this diploma is awarded, given under the hand of the President and the Secretary of the Senate."

Handing the diploma to Dr. Soendoro, he then added: "Allow me to be the first to congratulate you on the degree you have just received."

The hall rang with the shouts of the students and the applause of the guests. The President congratulated the new doctor of medicine and the adjutant brought in the mace. Then the name of Dr. Soendoro was added to those who had already been promoted. This was the first time in the history of Airlangga University that a candidate had been successfully promoted by a foreign professor, and it was a great honour both for my husband and for the World Health Organization.

Interestingly enough Dr. Soendoro had been a doctor before the promotion, but now he gained an additional privilege, for instead of using the title, Soendoro, dr. med., he was allowed to write, Soendoro, Dr. med. The capital made all the difference.

After the professors left the hall, the adjutant escorted Dr. Soendoro to his wife and together they walked into the library, where a reception was being held for them. The guests congratulated Dr. and Mrs. Soendoro and then broke into groups, talking, eating cakes and drinking the inevitable orange crush. During this interlude, the Dean of the Law School, as lean and gaunt as Cassius and with a wife as beautiful as Rosalind, came over to us and said: "I know you are leaving today. I just wanted to tell you that I hope you will be blessed with all the good things that God can offer you."

Soon thereafter, the President beckoned to me. When I walked over to him he placed a long envelope in my hand. "This is for you."

"Shall I open it now?" I asked.

"Yes, please do."

In the envelope there was a photograph that had been taken in 1920. It showed a group of students at the Hogere Burger School in Surabaja. In the picture there were twenty-seven boys and one girl, all of high-school age. Among them was President Pringgodigdo and Bung Karno who was wearing Indonesian dress. Those students had joined together to form the "Young Java Movement", one of the first such organizations to strive for national independence. From this small group came many of the national leaders of present-day Indonesia. When I tried to thank the President, he just shook his head and walked away.

Returning home we found our friend, Sampuran Singh, the Indian Consul in Surabaja, waiting impatiently. He was sure that we would miss the plane. In addition to his car there was another from the medical college, so there was room for all of us as well as Siti, Pappa, Manis and Sumiyati.

When we arrived at the airport the small restaurant there was crowded with friends and colleagues, who filled my arms with orchids. As my husband was still wearing his tuxedo, we looked like newly weds.

The last person to whom I said good-bye was Siti. Because she took such good care of us, I had time to write about Indonesia, this troubled paradise which has become one of the leading countries in world affairs.

Finally, having said good-bye to everyone, we went on to the airfield. Like the Hindu god Shiva we were leaving on a Garuda.

Index

Abednanon, Mrs., 57
Achmad, Police Brigadier, 74
"Adat" law, 53
Aden, 27
Affandi, 170
Afghanistan, 26
Africa, 176
Afro-Asian Hotel, 143
Agung, Sultan of Mataram, 172-3
Airlangga, King, 134
Airlangga University, 10, 38-9, 133-4, 184-5
Algeria, 26
al-Khindi, 181
All-Indonesian Importers Congress, 177
Ambon, 10, 43, 169, 171
America, *see* United States
Amoy, 174
Amsterdam, 129
Ananda, 124
Arabs, *see* Muslims
Arjuna, 12
Art in Indonesia, 151 ff.
Association of Indonesian Women, 57
Atjeh, 53
Atjehnese, 99
Aung San, 17
Australia, 26, 63, 70, 86, 94, 160
Averroes, 181

Badung, Raja of, 158
Bahasa Indonesia, 116, 139-40, 169-70, 182
Balai Pemuda, *see* Simpang Club
Bali, 10, 15, 31, 40, 54, 105, 108-9, 111, 134, 140, 141-61
Bali Hotel, 146
Banares, 124
Bandjuwanggi, 143
Bandung, 21, 24-6, 76, 113, 129-31
    Congress, 26
    Study Club, 18
    Technical School, 18
Bangka, 171
Banten, 14, 29, 35
Barong, 154-5

Bataks, 48, 54, 99
Batavia, 15, 21, 67, 136, 172-3
Bathok, Mount, 106-7
Batur, 111
Bedulu, 156
Beethoven, Ludwig van, 42, 170
Belgium, 99
Bengal, 139
Bhoma, 149
"Bhinneka Tunggal Ika", 115
Biliton, 171
Bima, 18
Bintang Timur, 74
Birnie, George, 66
Bligh, Captain William, 15
Bogor, 21, 24, 131
    Botanical Garden, 22, 24
    Pharmacology Laboratory, 22
    Veterinary Institute, 22, 24
Bolivia, 71
Bona, 156
Borneo, *see* Kalimantan
Borobudur, 113, 118, 120-8
Boston, Mass., 129
Bounty, H.M.S., 15
Boven Digul, 67, 78, 98
Brahma, 108
Brahmans, 108-9, 149-50
Brantas River, 37
Bromo, 103, 105-10, 112
Brueghel, 170
Brussels Congress (1927), 97
Buddha, 107, 109, 112, 121, 123-9
Buddhists, 28, 53-4, 107-8, 112, 121, 124, 180
"Budi Utomo", the, 138
Buitenzorg, 21-2
Bukit Tinggi, 97, 102
Bung Karno, *see* Sukarno, President
Burma, 26-8, 121, 176

California, University of, 137
Caltex Company, 101
Cambodia, 121
Carpenters' Union, New Jersey, *quoted*, 132

Celebes, *see* Sulawesi
Central Drug Research Institute, 9
Ceylon, 26, 121–2, 176
Chairil Anwar, 163
Chatter Manzil Palace, 9
Cheribon, *see* Tjirebon
Chiang Kai-shek, 171
China, 14–15, 66, 122, 158, 167, 169–78
Chinese, the, *see* China
Chou En-lai, 26
Climate, 10
Clothing, 31–2
Coen, Jan Pieterszoon, 30, 35, 172
Communist Party, *see* Partai Komunis
    Indonesia
Cook, Captain, 15, 22, 136, 173
Covarrubias, Miguel, 145, 157–8
Cremation ceremonies, 141–3, 149–50
Cricket and Lawn Tennis Club, 86

Daendals, Herman Willem, 35–6, 90, 174
Dances, 154–7; *see also* Ketjak Dance;
    Sarampang Duabelas; Serimpi Dance
Darul Islam, 75–7, 92
Darwin, Charles, 181
Day of National Awakening, 138
Dekker, E. Douwes, 89
    E. F. E. Douwes, 91
de Kock, General, 118
Deli, 67
Denpasar, 134, 143, 146, 150, 154, 159–61
Devi, 108
Dewi Sri, 37
De Zeven Provincien, 68
Diponegoro, Prince, 36, 117–19
Disease, 135–7
Djajaprana, 143
Djambek, 94
Djepara, Regent of, 131
Djogodolok, 180
Djuanda, Prime Minister, 92
Djuhir Mohammed, 102
Draupadi, 104
Drona, *quoted*, 121
Dulles, John F., 63, 95
Dutch, the, 11–15, 17–22, 24–6, 29, 35–6,
    56, 61–72, 75, 78–102, 117–20, 126,
    130–6, 157–8, 168–9, 171–5, 178, 182;
    see also Royal Dutch Airlines; Royal
    Dutch Oil Company; Royal Dutch
    Packet Shipping Lines

Early society, 22

East Java Body for Co-operation between
    Women and the Military, 50
Economic measures, 159–67
Education, 130–5, 138–40
    Conference, Bandung, 129, 130 ff.
    Ministry of, 113, 132, 135
Egypt, 26
Ethiopia, 26
Eurasians, status of, 89–90

Faculty of Education, Malang, 134
Fakultas Gigi, Surabaja, 39
Fakultas Hukum, Surabaja, 38
Fakultas Kedokteran, Surabaja, 10, 39, 45,
    62, 80, 91, 137, 140, 177, 181–3
Fiji Islands, 176
Flores, 10, 15, 18
Forge of Vulcan, 111
France, 99
French Indo-China, 176
From Darkness to Light (Kartini), 57
Fukien province, China, 174

Gadjah Mada, Prime Minister of Madja-
    pahit, 114–15
    University, 116, 133
Gado-gado, 59
Galdo, G. Q., 71
Gandhi, Mahatma, 17
Ganesh, 114
Ganto Suaro, 102
Garuda Indonesia Airlines, 79, 162
Gauguin, 141
Gautama, *see* Buddha
General Assembly, *see* United Nations
Ghaziuddin Haider, Nawab, 9
Gilimanuk, 144, 160
Gillespie, Major-General, 117
Glodok, 15–16
Gomati River, 9
Great Britain, 10, 78, 99, 153
Gresik, 179
Gujarat, 179
Gunung Batur, 111
Gurkas, 93
Gusti Daradjatun, Prince, *see* Hamengku
    Buwono IX

Hadji Bahauddin, 67
Hadjis, 75
Hamengku Buwono IX, Sultan of Jogja-
    karta, 58, 92, 98, 118–20

Harvard University, 170
Hasan Udin, Sultan, 102
Hassan, 106–7, 109
Hatta, Mohammed, 75, 92, 97–8, 100
Hayam Wuruk, King, 114–15
Heroes' Monument, the, 37
Hinduism, 28, 40, 53–4, 108, 115, 126, 130, 134, 148, 180
Hindus, 108, 112, 138, 154, 180
Hiranyavati River, 124
Ho Chi-minh, President, 97, 144
Holland, see Dutch, the
Hogere Burger School, 18, 185
Horsfield, Dr. Thomas, 24
Hussein, Lt.-Col. Ahmad, 92, 94, 96
Hutasoit, M., 132
Huxley, T. H., 181

Imhoff, Willem van, 21
India, 10, 12, 14, 26–7, 52, 88, 122–4, 141–2, 176, 179
Indische society, 21–2
Indonesia Accuses, 18
Indonesia, University of, 137
Indonesian Association, 97
"Indos", 89
Indra, 145, 162
Infant mortality, 46
International Congress for Peace, 26
Iran, 26
Iraq, 26
Irian Barat, 61, 63–6, 68–73, 77–8, 80, 91, 100, 164
Islam, 56, 75, 108, 115, 130

Jangalla, 114
Japan, 14, 25, 58, 68, 80, 90, 98, 136–7, 139, 158, 163, 168, 170–1; see also World War II
Jasbir Singh, 108–9
Java, 10 ff., 100, 103–6, 108, 115 ff., 124, 126–8, 131, 133–4, 143, 145–6, 148, 151–3, 161, 164, 168–9, 174, 179, 181–2
Java Modemagazyn, 84
Jogjakarta, 12, 36, 57, 68, 80, 92, 113, 115–20, 133–4, 137–8, 163, 169, 182
Juwitha, 106–7

Kalimantan, 10, 15, 108, 171
Kampungs, 16–17, 38, 45–7, 59, 69, 151, 183
Kartini, Raden Adjing, 56–7, 131
Kasada ceremony, 103–4, 109, 147

Kebajoran, 15
Kediri, 114
Kemajoran Airport, 72, 80
Ketjak dance-drama, 156–7
Khrushchev, Nikita, 116
KLM, see Royal Dutch Airlines
Kongres Wanita Indonesia, 58, 133
"Kopi Tobruk", 105
Korea, 96
KPM, see Royal Dutch Packet Shipping Lines
Krakatau, 111
Krishna, 12, 18, 114
Kshatriyas, 143, 149–50
Kusinagara, 121
Kusomo, 109–10

Lakshmi, 114
Lampungs, 99
Language, 116, 139–40; see also Bahasa Indonesia; Sanscrit
Lebanon, 26
Lebaran, 181
Lenya, Lotte, 9
Leyden Museum, 128
Literacy, 139
Local People's Council of Representatives, 120
Lombok, 15, 54, 157
London, 80, 129
Losman Sukapura Pension, 103–4, 111
Lubis, 94, 96
Lucknow, 9–11
Lumbini Gardens, 125

Madiun, 75–6, 163
Madjapahit Empire, 35, 108–9, 114–15, 134
Madras, 176
Madrid, 111
Madura, 96
Magelang, 118
Mahabharata, the, 12, 18, 104, 148
Makassar, 101–2, 158
Malang, 134
Malaya, 139, 176
Mallas of Kusinagara, the, 121
Manis, see Yanto
Man Ti Ko, 174
Marriage customs, 53–6
Malik, Ibrahim, 179, 181
Mara, 125
Martandang ceremony, 54
Mas, 153

Masjumi Party, 75, 91, 97–8, 164
Mataram, 29–30, 34, 36
Max Havelaar (Dekker), 89
Maya, Queen, 125
McLeod, Lt.-Col., 117
Mecca, 75
Medicine, 135–8
Menado, 101
Merauke, 80
Merdeka Palace, 18, 20, 49
Minangkubaus, 53, 99
Minto, Elliot, 88
Mohammed Adbuh, Mufti Sheikh, 56
Mohammedanism, *see* Islam
Mohammed, Police Adjunct-Inspector, 74
Moluccas, 15
Montreal, 80
Morocco, 26
Moscow, 17
Multatuli, *see* Dekker, E. Douwes
"Musjawarat", 92
Muslims, 9, 11, 16, 18, 53–4, 67, 99, 102,
    115, 138, 143, 148, 164, 179–81

Nahdatul Ulama Party, 76, 164
Napoleon, 35
Nasution, Maj.-Gen. Harris, 79, 93, 165
Nationale Indische Partij, 91
NATO, 65
Nehru, Jawaharlal, 17, 26, 52, 97
Nepal, 123
Netherlands, *see* Dutch, the
Netherlands Indies, 11
New Delhi, 17, 26
New Guinea, *see* Irian Barat
New York, 10–11, 105
Ngadisari, 104–5, 111
Nirvana, 125–6
Noormathias, Major, 102

Oil, 100
Oleg, 154
Oltmans, William L., 72
Omar Khayyám, 181
"Operation August 17th", 102
Oranje Hotel, Surabaja, 39

Padang, 92, 96, 102
Painting, 151–3
Paken Baru, 101
Pakistan, 26
Paku Alam, 139

Pantja Sila, the, 74–5, 133
Pantjasila Seminar, 163
Pappa, 41, 43, 186
Paris, 17, 129
Partai Komunis Indonesia, 50, 66–8, 120,
    164
Partai Nasional Indonesia, 18, 164
Pekalongan, 29
Persia, 14
Philippines, 26, 101, 176
PKI, 175
Pope, Albert Lawrence, 102
Prambanan, the, 126
Pringgodigdo, President A. G., 134, 184–5
Probolinggo, 103, 174, 184
Prostitution, 53
Puasa, 179
"Puteri Merdeka", 57

Quinine, 24–5

Raden Paku, *see* Sunan Giri
Raffles, Sir Stamford, 36, 117, 126
Raffles Hotel, Singapore, 101
Ramadan, 179
Ramayana, the, 42, 148
Rangda, 155
Rangoon, 9, 13, 17
Rauwolfia Serpentina, 22
Rembang, Regent of, 57
Rembrandt, 30
Renville Truce, 169
"River Solo, The", 81
Rockefeller, John D., 100
Rockefeller Foundation, 153
Roosevelt, F. D., 15
Rosella, 139
Rotterdam, 97, 102
Round Table Conference, The Hague
    (1949), 65, 98
Rousseau, Henri, 152
Royal Dutch Airlines, 79
Royal Dutch Oil Company, 100
Royal Dutch Packet Shipping Lines, 14, 79,
    81
Rubber, 99–100
Rubens, 170
Rumah Sakit Umum Pusat, 45

Sabang, 80
Saigon, 13
Sailendra kings, 121, 127

Salatiga, 29–31
Sampurah Singh, 185
Sanghyang Ibu Pretiwi, 145
Sanscrit, 108, 116, 147–8
Sanitation, 136
Sanur, 146, 158–60
Sarampang Duabelas Dance, 22
Sasak, 102
Saudi Arabia, 26
Sculpture, 153–4
SEATO, 63, 98
Security Council, see United Nations
Selecta, 168
Sekolah Menak, 131
Sekolah Radja, 131
Semarang, 28–9, 117, 126
Serimpi Dance, 34
Setibugghi, see Dekker, E. F. E. Douwes
Shaftesbury, Lord, quoted, 180
Shantiniketan, Bengal, 139
Shiva, 108, 134, 186
Siam, 128
Siddhartha, see Buddha
Sikhs, 93
Simbolon, 94, 96
Simpang Club, 80–2
Singapore, 21, 79, 93–5, 98–101
Singaradja, 143
Siti, 41–3, 49–50, 62, 116–17, 162, 183, 186
Sjafruddin Prawiranegara, 92, 96–7
Smeru, Mount, 106–7
SOBSI, 65, 68–9
Soegeng, B., 151–4, 160–1, 183
Soendoro, Dr., 181, 183–5
   Mrs., 183, 185
Soetan Sjahrir, 152
   quoted, 25
Solo, 33–7, 54, 58, 117
Solo, Prince of, 55
Soviet Union, 78, 116
Spoor, General, 119
Standard Oil Company of New Jersey, 100
Stupas, 113, 121–2
Subriando, Dr. Hurustiati, 52–3, 58, 68, 70–2
Sudarto, Major, 74
Sudras, 149–50
Sujata, 126
Sukapura, 103
Sukarno, Guntur, 74
   Megawati, 74
   Njonja Fatmawati, 49–51
   President, 17–20, 22, 26, 28, 36, 47,

49–52, 62, 70, 74–6, 80, 92, 94, 97–8, 131, 134–5, 140, 151, 162–5, 169, 182, 185
Sulawesi, 10, 15, 93, 101–2, 137
Suluh Indonesia, 77
Sumatra, 10, 15, 18, 43, 48, 53–4, 66–7, 92–3, 95–103, 105, 108, 120, 131, 137, 169, 171, 174
Sumatran Youth Movement, 97
Sumiyati, 43–4, 50, 76, 86
Sunan Giri, 179–81
Surabaja, 9–11, 18, 37–9, 46–7, 49–50, 54, 60, 73, 80, 83, 87, 92, 95, 96, 99, 101, 111–13, 131, 133–4, 137–8, 140, 143, 151, 160, 162, 164–6, 170, 177–8, 180, 183, 185; Darmo area, 38, 62–3
"Surabaja Johnny", 9
Surakarta, see Solo
Suwardi Surjaningrat, Raden Mas, 138–9
Syria, 26

Taboos, 40–1
Tagore, Rabindranath, 139
Taiwan, 95, 101, 171
"Taman Siswa", 139
Tanah Merah, see Boven Digul
Tandjung Priok, 16
Tegal, 29
Tengger Mountains, 106, 109
Tenggerese, 106, 108–10
Tennyson, Alfred Lord, 111
Ter Poorten, Lt.-Gen., 25
Texas, 10, 39, 168
Thailand, 121, 136
Tiga Dara, 24
Timor, 10, 15
Tito, Marshal, 38
Tjirebon, 27–8, 36, 40
Tjikini Elementary School, 74, 77, 94
Tjokroaminoto, Raden, 131
Tjou Eng, Dr., 168
Tosari village, 103
Trade Union Movement, 66–9
Traffic, 31–2
Transaera Hotel Djakarta, 13, 29, 77–8
Trawulan, 114
Tretes, 73
Tuak, 21
Tuban, Regent of, 134
Tunisia, 26
Turkey, 14

Ubud, 172

Udayana Literary Faculty, 134, 140
Uncle Tom's Cabin (Stowe), 89
Ungaran, 118
United Nations, 21, 26, 62–3, 65, 70–3, 77–8, 169
United States, 65, 78, 95, 98–9, 132, 153, 168, 171
United States Rubber Company, 99
U Nu, 17
Utusan Hindia, 18

Vaisyas, 115, 149–50
van der Wijck, C. H. J., 128
Vietnam, 96
Voltaire, 181

Wahidin Sudirohusodo, Dr., 138–9
Washington, D.C., 17
Wayang Kulit, 147–8, 155
Wayang Orang, 179
Westerling, Captain Raymond, 102, 158
West Irian, *see* Irian Barat
West New Guinea, *see* Irian Barat

Wijono, Njonja, 50
Wisnu, 145
Women, status of, 51–8
World Health Organization, 9–10, 76–7, 137, 181, 185
World War I, 66
World War II, 24–5, 58, 68, 90, 136–7, 168, 176, 182

Yacht Club, 182
Yale Medical School, 181
Yanto, 41, 43, 186
Yasodhara, 125
Yemen, 26–7
Young Ambon Group, 43
Young Indonesia, 43
Young Java Group, 18, 43, 185
Young Sumatra Group, 43
Youth Day, 43–4

Zaman, Dr., 182
Zangrandi, 62
Zorach, William, 153

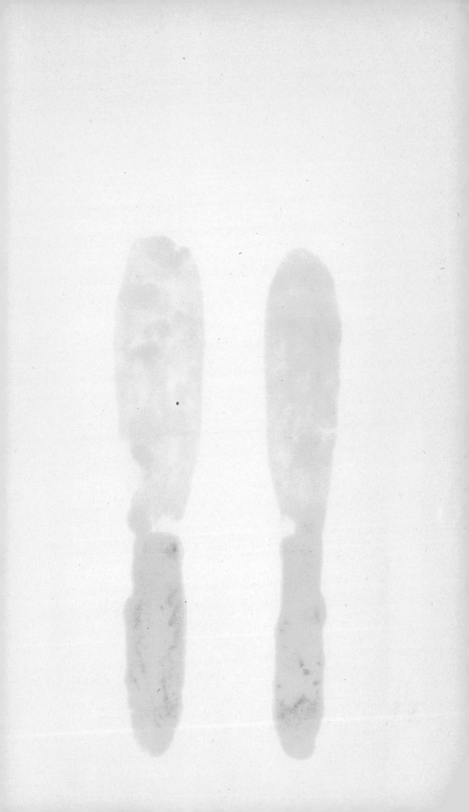

9/63

DATE DUE

GAYLORD

PRINTED IN U.S.A.

F